SMART SKETCH BOOK 5

Oogie Art's step-by-step guide to drawing facial features in charcoal and pastel.

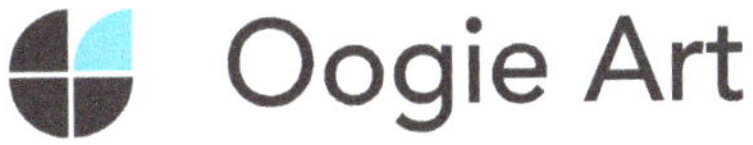

Oogie Art's SmartSketchbook™
An Expert's Guide to Facial Features in Charcoal and Pastel
First Edition, Copyright © 2015

Produced and Edited by
Oogie Art
New York, NY

© Text
Oogie Art

© Photographs
Licensed under Oogie Art®

Directed by
Wook Choi

Assistant Directed by
Clara Lu

Drawings by
Jee Hwang

Tips by
Wook Choi

Published and Distributed by
Oogie Publishing House
New York, NY
www.oogiepublishinghouse.com
(212) 714-1011

All rights reserved. No part of this book covered by the copyright hereon may be reproduced, resold, or used in any form or by any means without written permission of the publisher.

ISBN 978-0-9855809-6-4
Printed in the United States

"Oogie Art" is a registered trademark of Oogie Art, Inc.

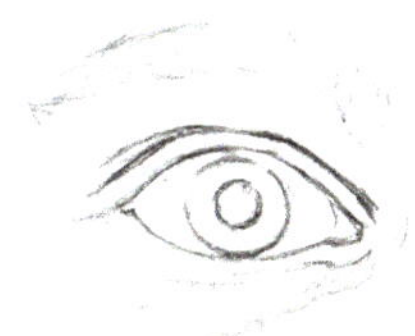 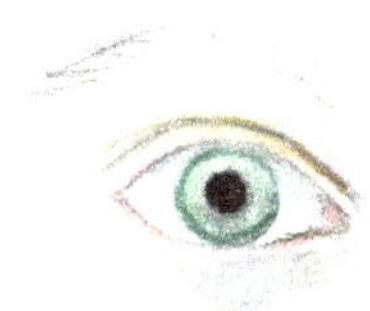 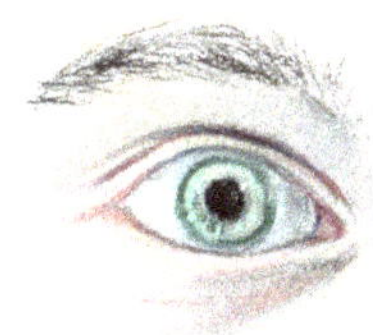 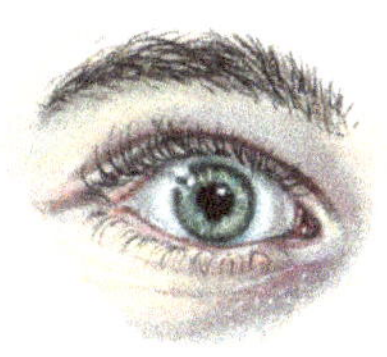

CONTENTS

Introduction to Pastel for Skin Tones

There will be no exact skin tone in your set of pastels. They must be built up by layering different colors. Do not limit yourself to peaches and browns for your skin tones. There are many blues, greens, purples, and reds in skin; colors that you can easily add in pastel.

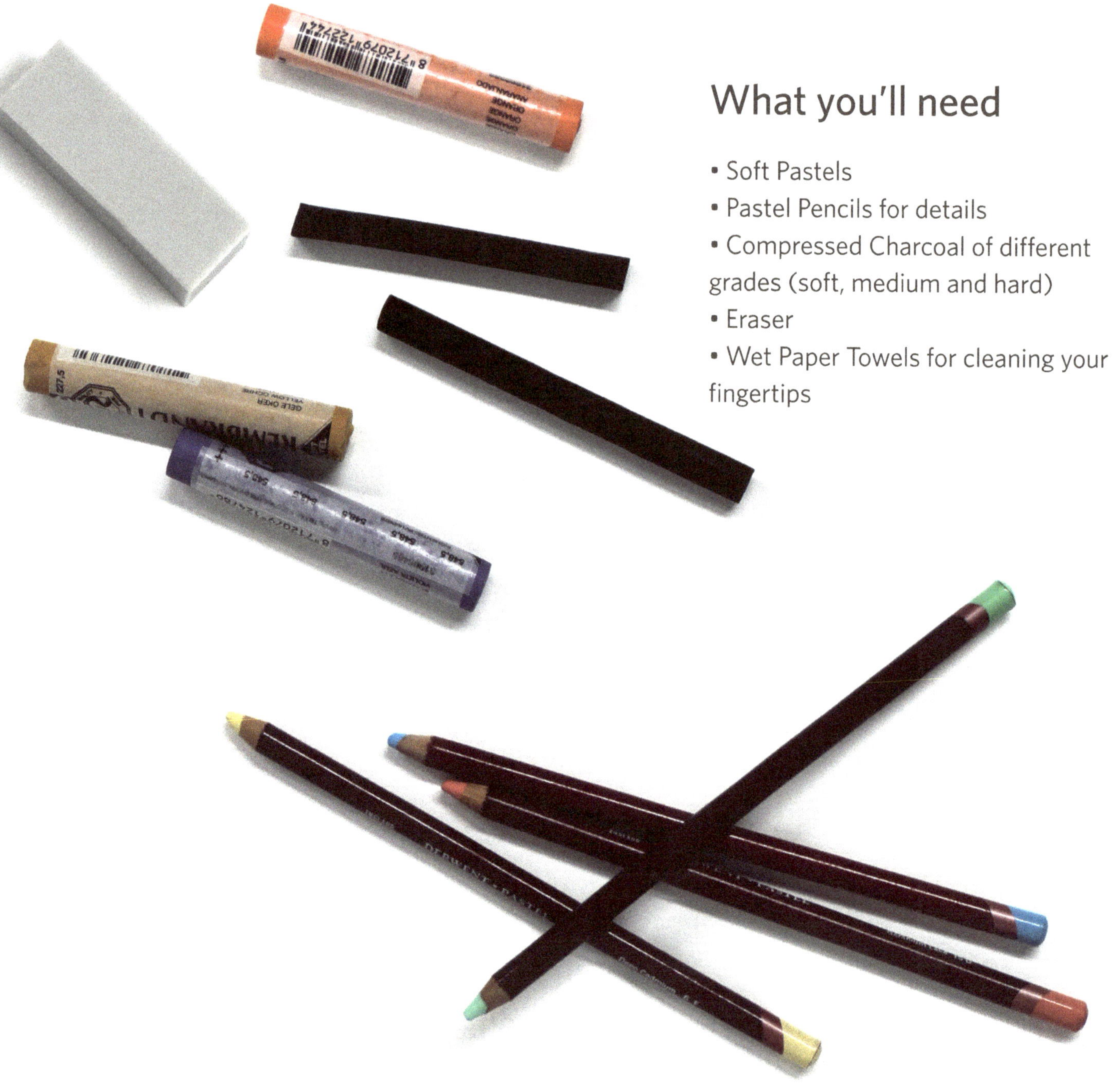

What you'll need

- Soft Pastels
- Pastel Pencils for details
- Compressed Charcoal of different grades (soft, medium and hard)
- Eraser
- Wet Paper Towels for cleaning your fingertips

Pastel Color Mixing Techniques

Blending and scumbling are great techniques for mixing color for skin tone. Start by lightly drawing an outline of the face and features. Once you're sure the proportions are correct, start blocking in your values. Experiment with different tones, from greens and blues, to oranges and purples. Then start layering your other colors, try using a yellow ochre, pink, light purple, yellow, and white for the highlights. Skin falling in shadows should have more browns and greens. Use more blue for sunken in areas, like the eyes and parts of the neck and collarbone. Remember to keep aware of the direction of your light source to keep your shading and values consistent.

Use a mixture of blending and scumbling to add more dimension to your drawing.

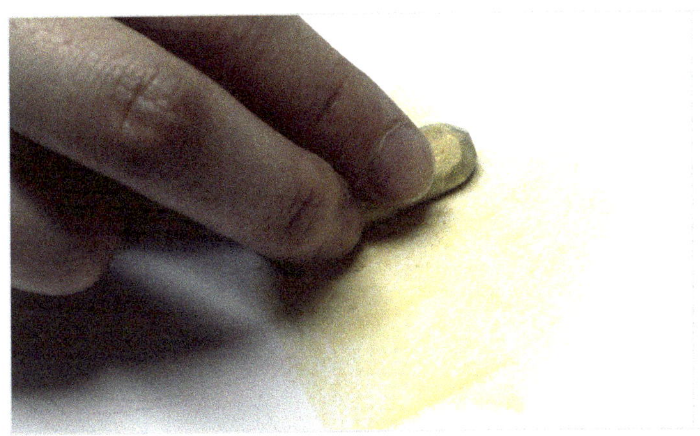

Layer line drawing on top to add details and create a more gestural and expressive quality.

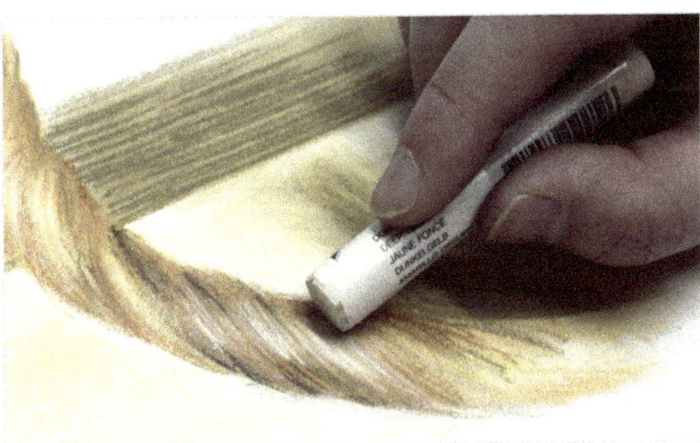

It can be very daunting for the beginning artist to start drawing a face. One of the most important things to remember is where your features (eyes, nose, and mouth) are positioned. Eyes are positioned right in the middle of the head. The nose ends at the midpoint between the chin and the eyes, while the mouth is halfway between the nose and chin. Another important aspect that many artists ignore are the planes of the face. The underlying structure of the skull and muscles determine the shape of our faces.

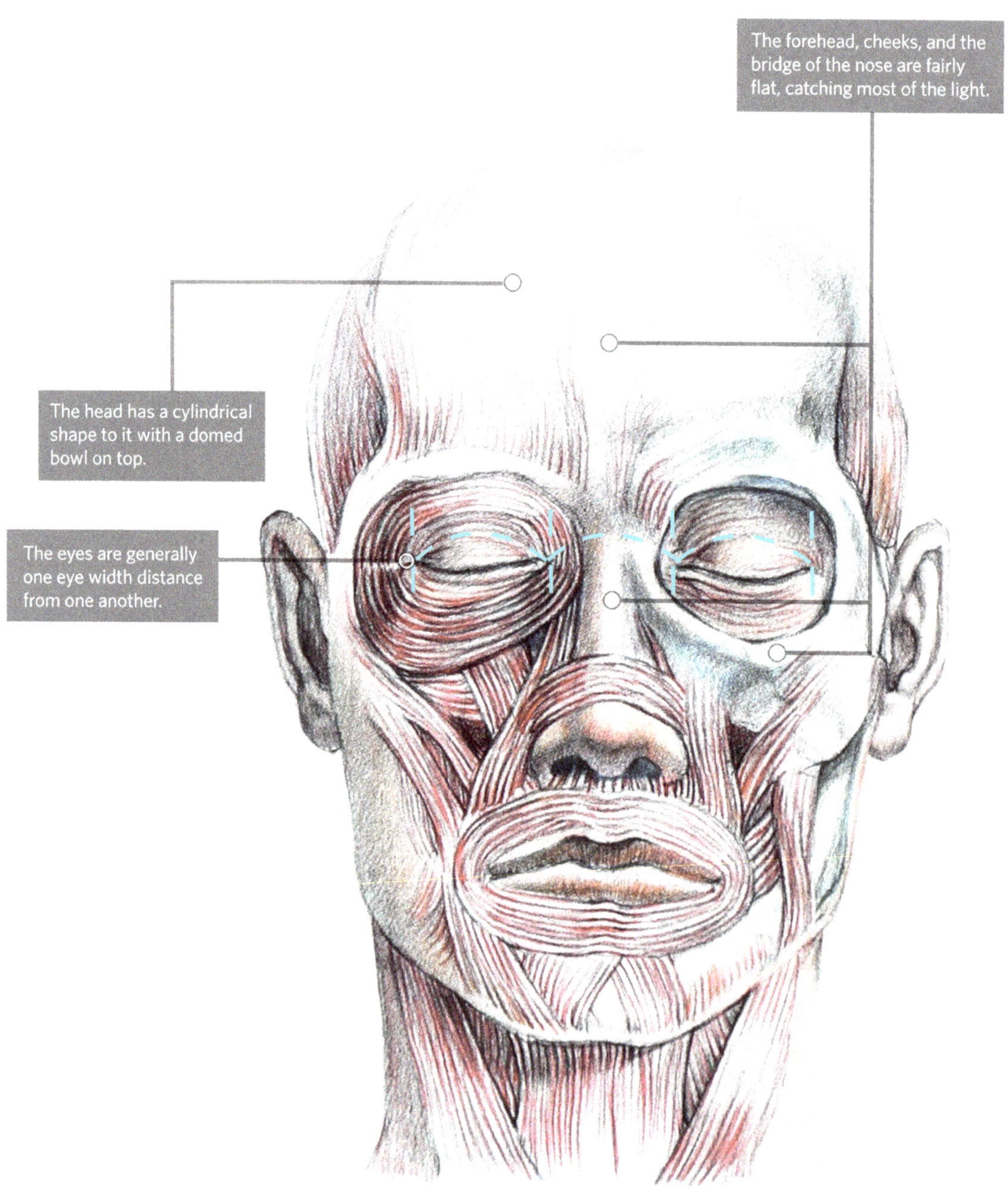

Now try drawing the face structure yourself.

In relation to the face, the eye is sunken in and the brow shades much of the eye. Areas that receive highlight are the eyelids, the outer region of the brow, and the upper cheek. Notice that the whites of the eyes are not really "white" but are in the shadows cast by the eyelids. Also note that the width of the iris about a third of the width of the eye itself.

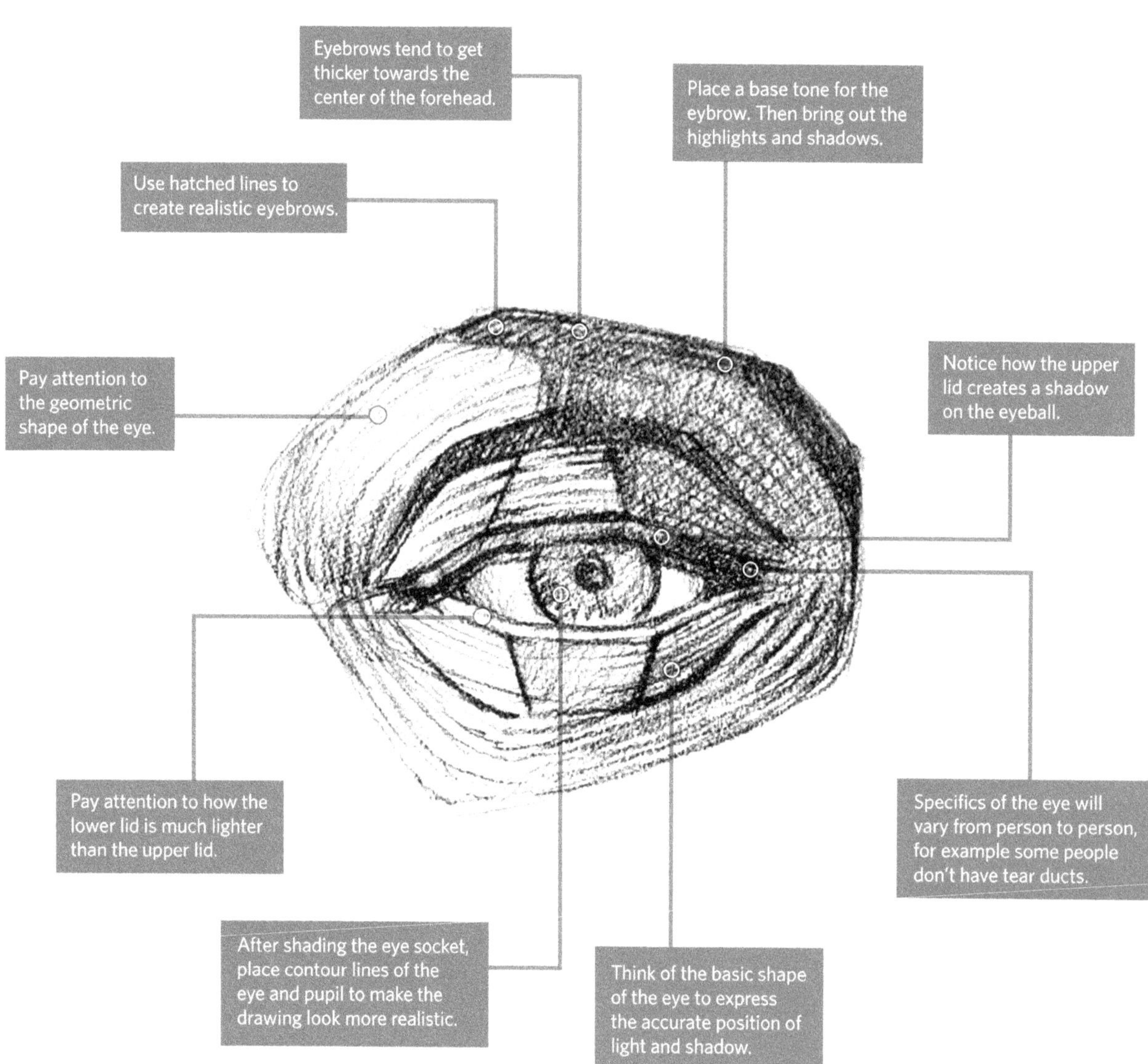

Now try drawing the eye yourself.

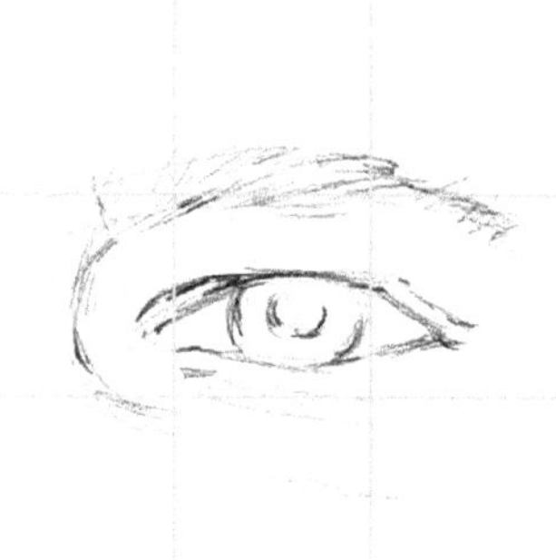

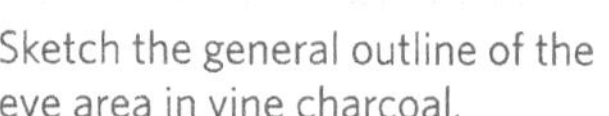

Sketch the general outline of the eye area in vine charcoal.

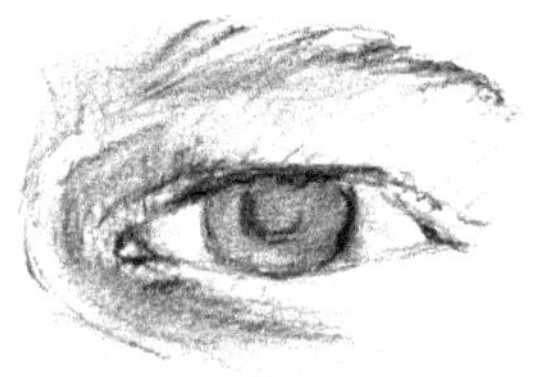

Begin to lightly shade in areas of shadow, eye muscles, and the pupil.

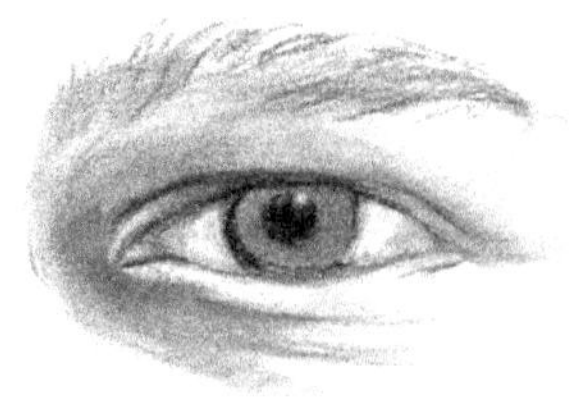

Pay attention to the volume created by shadow and light on the eye. Remember the entire eye area is a sunken area so most of it is in shadow.

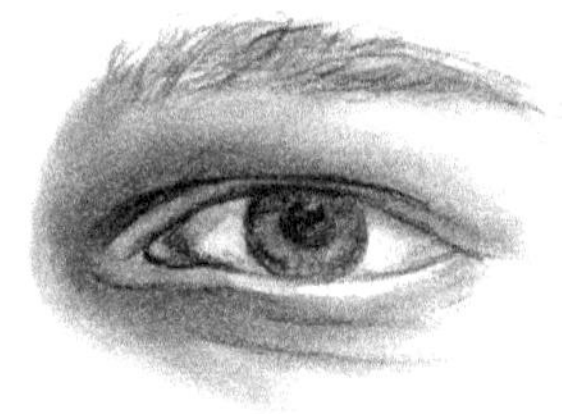

Continue to render the eye area and introduce some compressed charcoal for areas of extreme darkness.

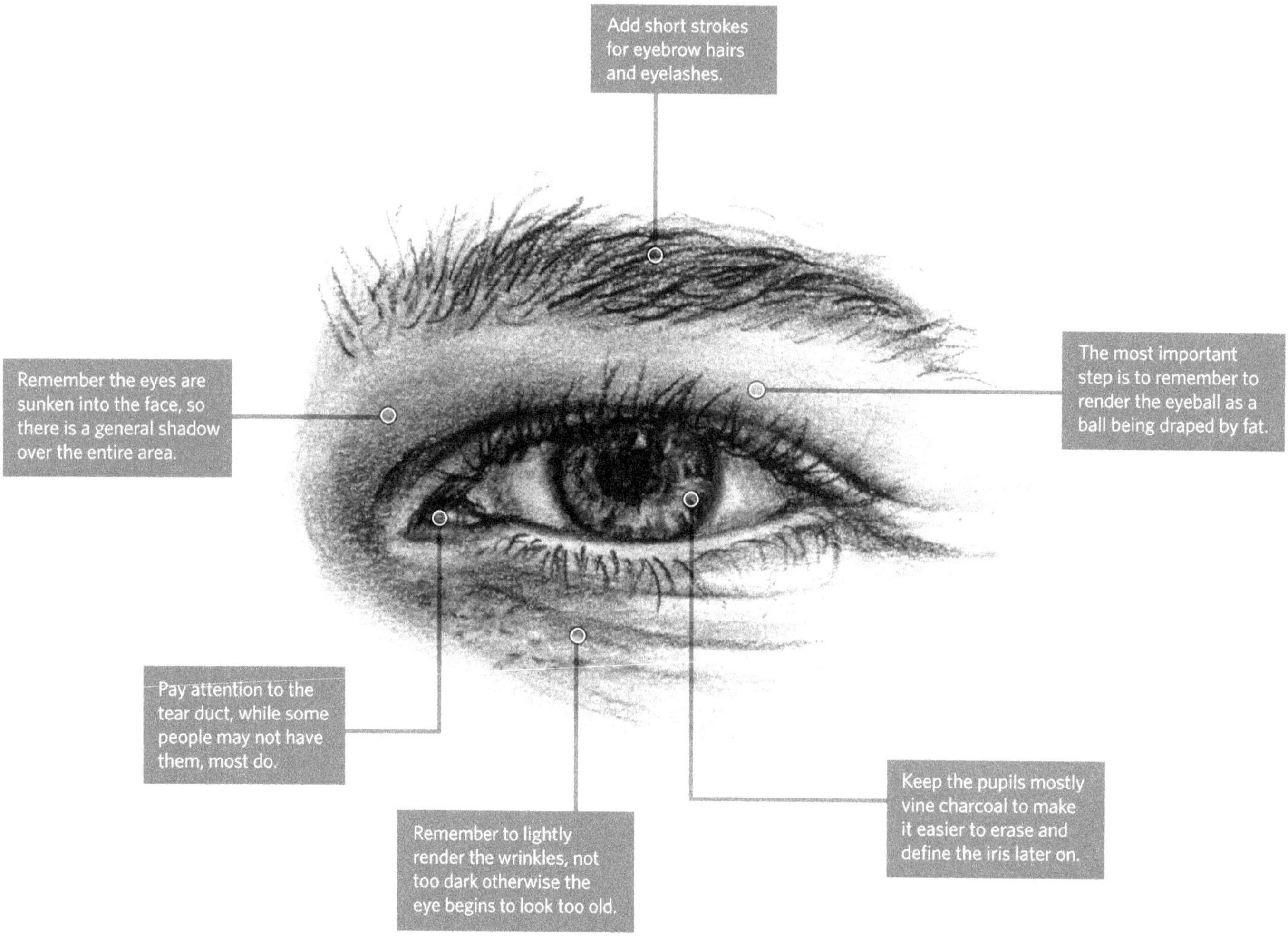

Add short strokes for eyebrow hairs and eyelashes.

Remember the eyes are sunken into the face, so there is a general shadow over the entire area.

The most important step is to remember to render the eyeball as a ball being draped by fat.

Pay attention to the tear duct, while some people may not have them, most do.

Keep the pupils mostly vine charcoal to make it easier to erase and define the iris later on.

Remember to lightly render the wrinkles, not too dark otherwise the eye begins to look too old.

Now try drawing the left eye yourself.

Now that you have practiced how to draw the left eye in charcoal following a step-by-step tutorial, use the page on the right to try and draw from life. You can draw from the picture below, use a mirror, or ask a friend to sit for you and try different variations of compositions.

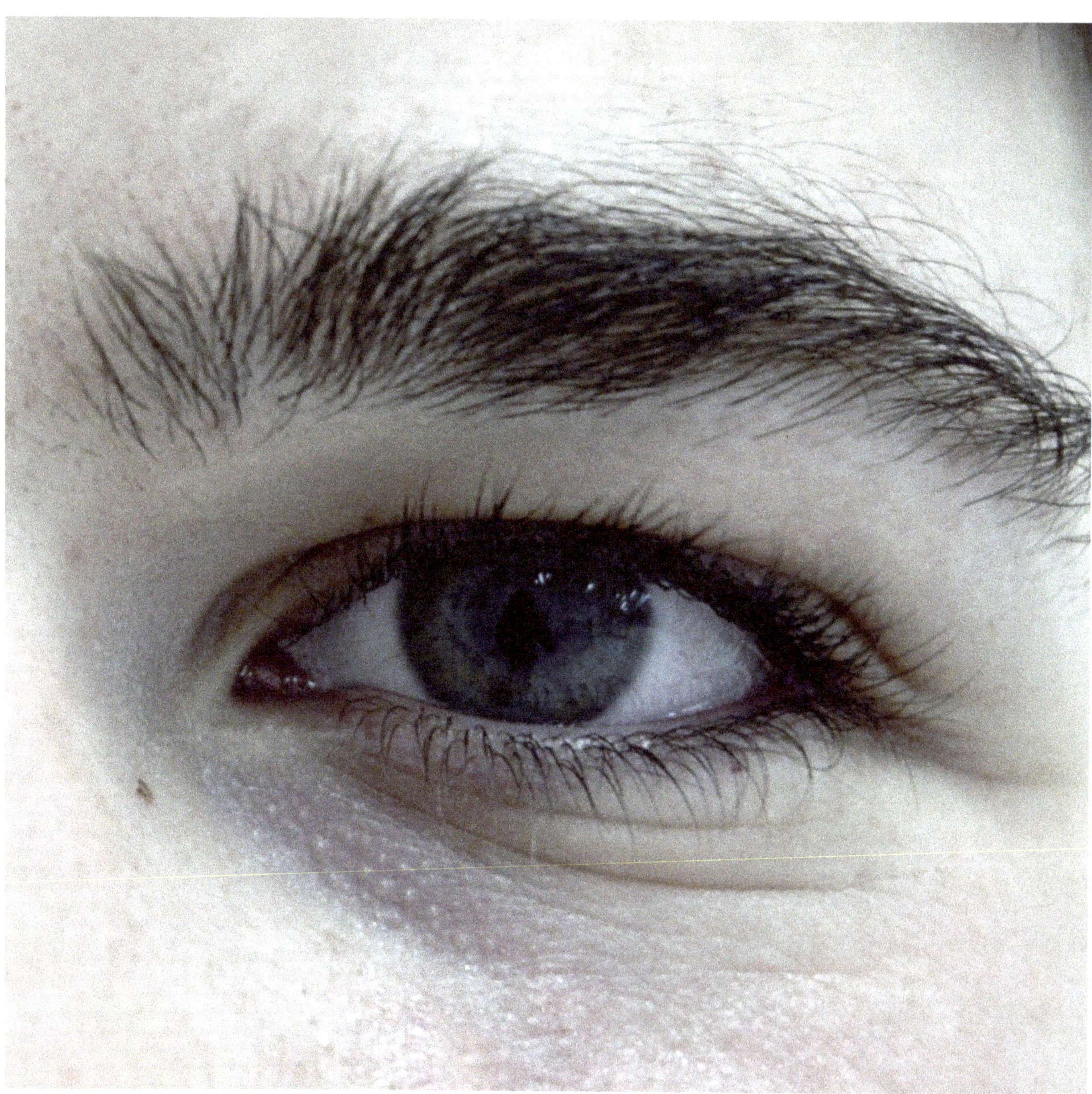

LEFT EYE IN CHARCOAL: PRACTICE II

Now try drawing the left eye yourself without the grid.

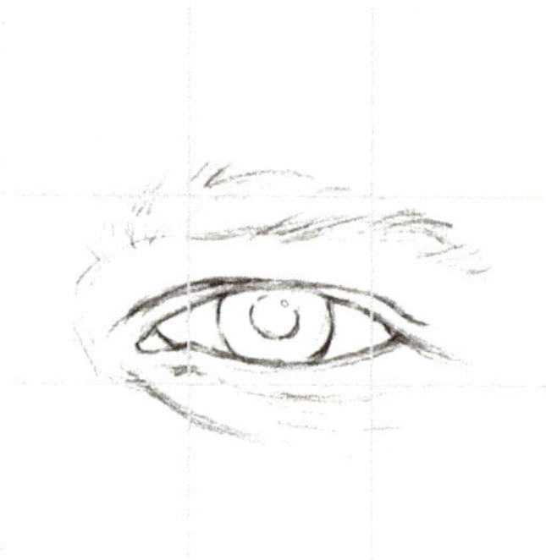
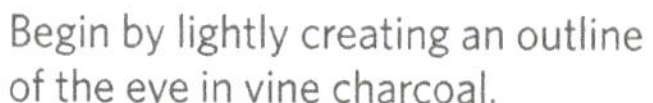

Begin by lightly creating an outline of the eye in vine charcoal.

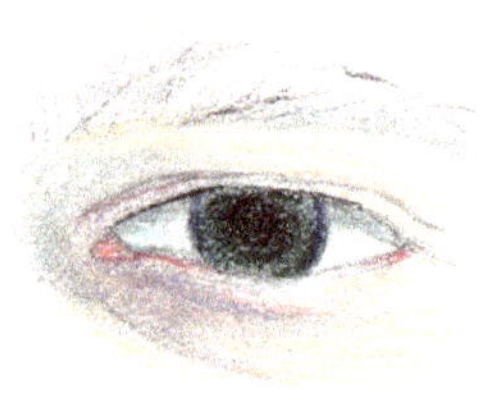

Lightly place the skin colors to cover the entire drawn area. Don't forget to add in a little bit of blues and pinks.

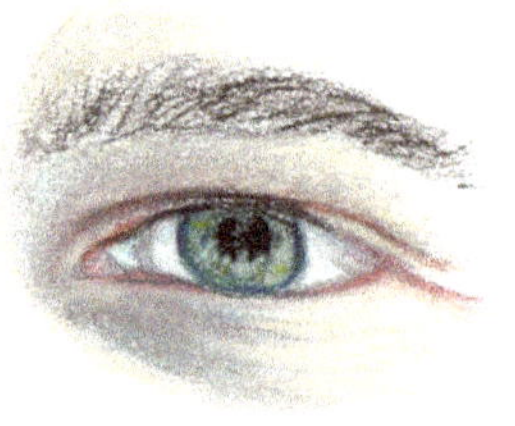

Blend in your colors and add in a variety of skin tones to richen your skin tone colors. Begin rendering the lights and shadows including general eyebrow hairs.

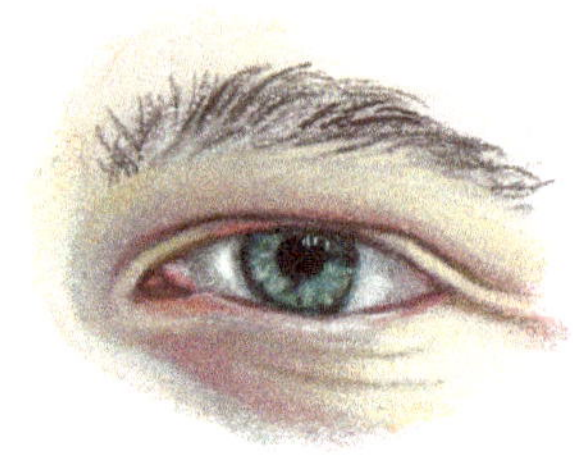

Continue rendering the volume and colors of the eye area. Save the small details, eyebrow hairs, eyelashes, eyeball highlights and iris details for the very end.

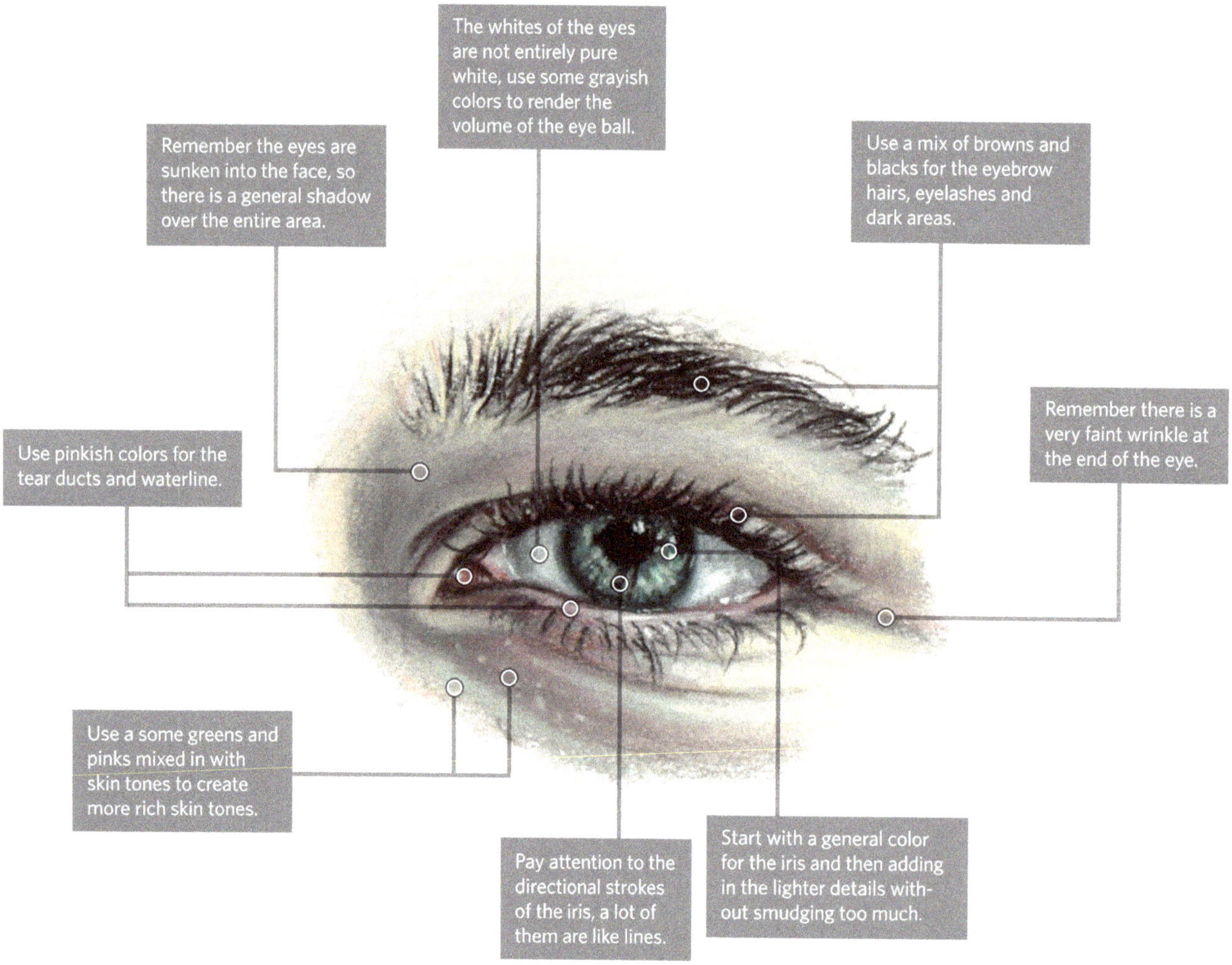

The whites of the eyes are not entirely pure white, use some grayish colors to render the volume of the eye ball.

Remember the eyes are sunken into the face, so there is a general shadow over the entire area.

Use a mix of browns and blacks for the eyebrow hairs, eyelashes and dark areas.

Use pinkish colors for the tear ducts and waterline.

Remember there is a very faint wrinkle at the end of the eye.

Use a some greens and pinks mixed in with skin tones to create more rich skin tones.

Pay attention to the directional strokes of the iris, a lot of them are like lines.

Start with a general color for the iris and then adding in the lighter details without smudging too much.

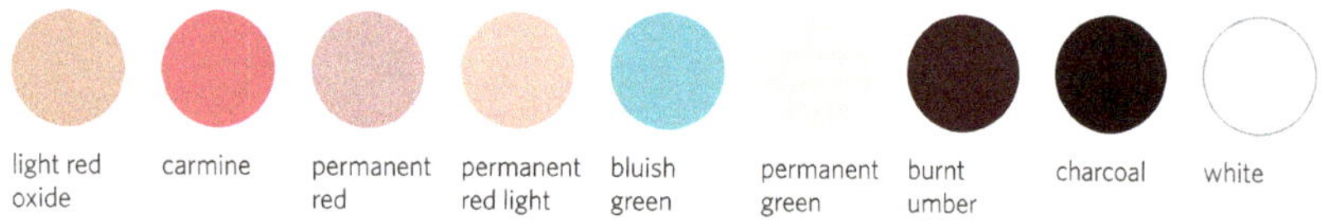

light red oxide

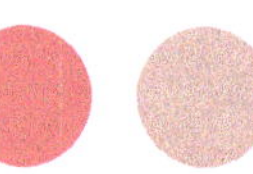
carmine

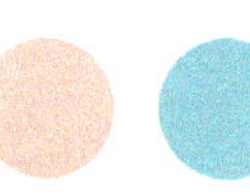
permanent red

permanent red light

bluish green

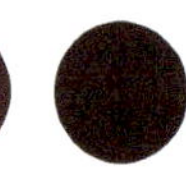
permanent green

burnt umber

charcoal

white

Now try drawing the eye yourself.

Now that you have practiced how to draw the left eye in pastel following a step-by-step tutorial, use the page on the right to try and draw from life. You can draw from the picture below, use a mirror, or ask a friend to sit for you and try different variations of compositions.

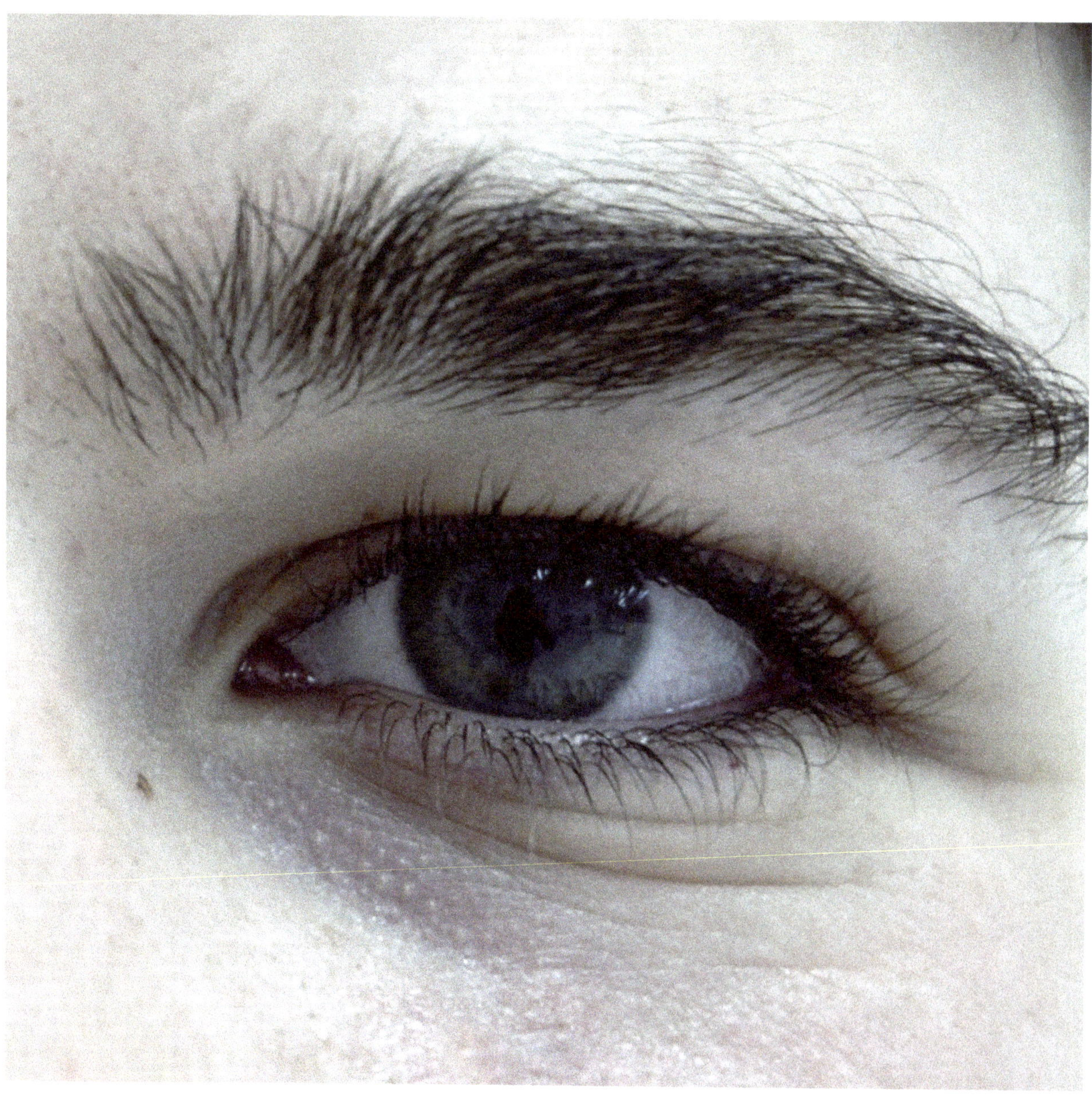

Now try drawing the left eye yourself without the grid.

SURPRISED RIGHT EYE IN CHARCOAL: TIPS

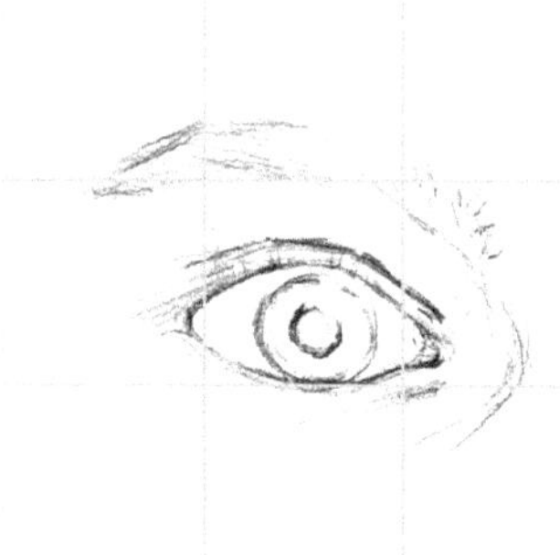

First sketch the general components of the eye area in vine charcoal.

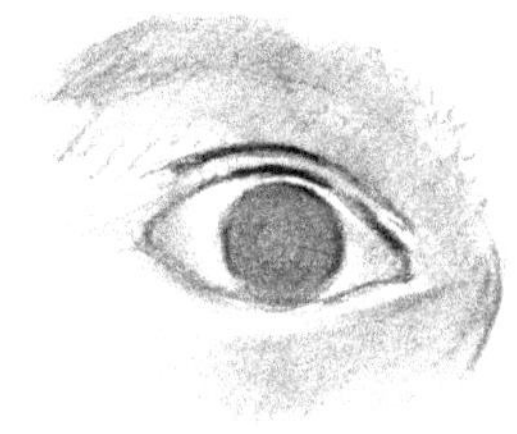

Block in the general areas of shadow, light and the iris.

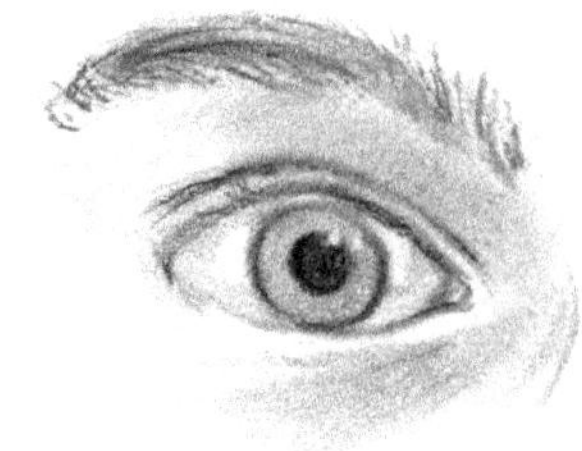

Identify the areas of light, shadow, and reflection light using smudging, shading, and erasing.

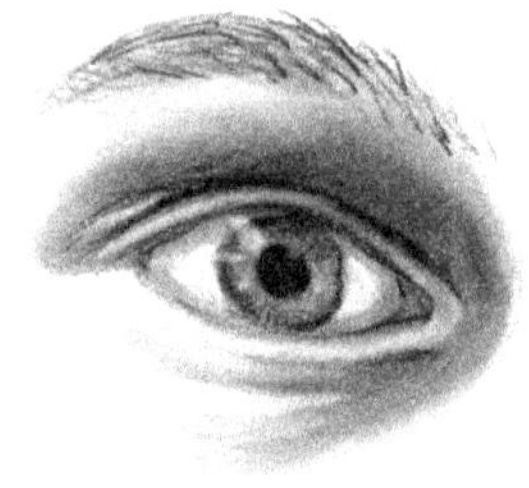

Continue to render the volume of the eye area, paying attention to how the eye sits within the eye socket and how the flesh sits around the eyeball.

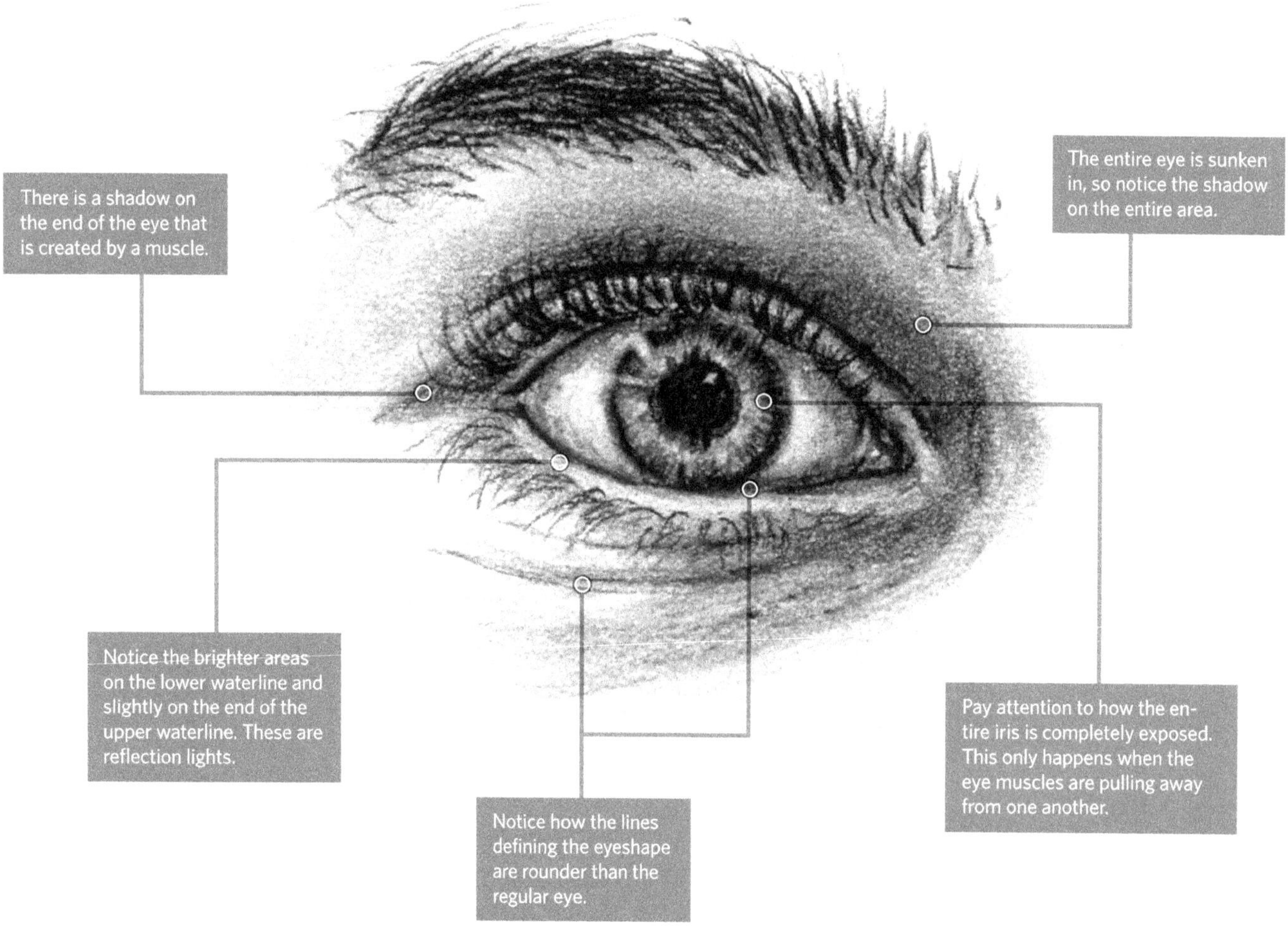

There is a shadow on the end of the eye that is created by a muscle.

The entire eye is sunken in, so notice the shadow on the entire area.

Notice the brighter areas on the lower waterline and slightly on the end of the upper waterline. These are reflection lights.

Notice how the lines defining the eyeshape are rounder than the regular eye.

Pay attention to how the entire iris is completely exposed. This only happens when the eye muscles are pulling away from one another.

Now try drawing the surprised right eye yourself.

Now that you have practiced how to draw a surprised right eye in charcoal following a step-by-step tutorial, use the page on the right to try and draw from life. You can draw from the picture below, use a mirror, or ask a friend to sit for you and try different variations of compositions.

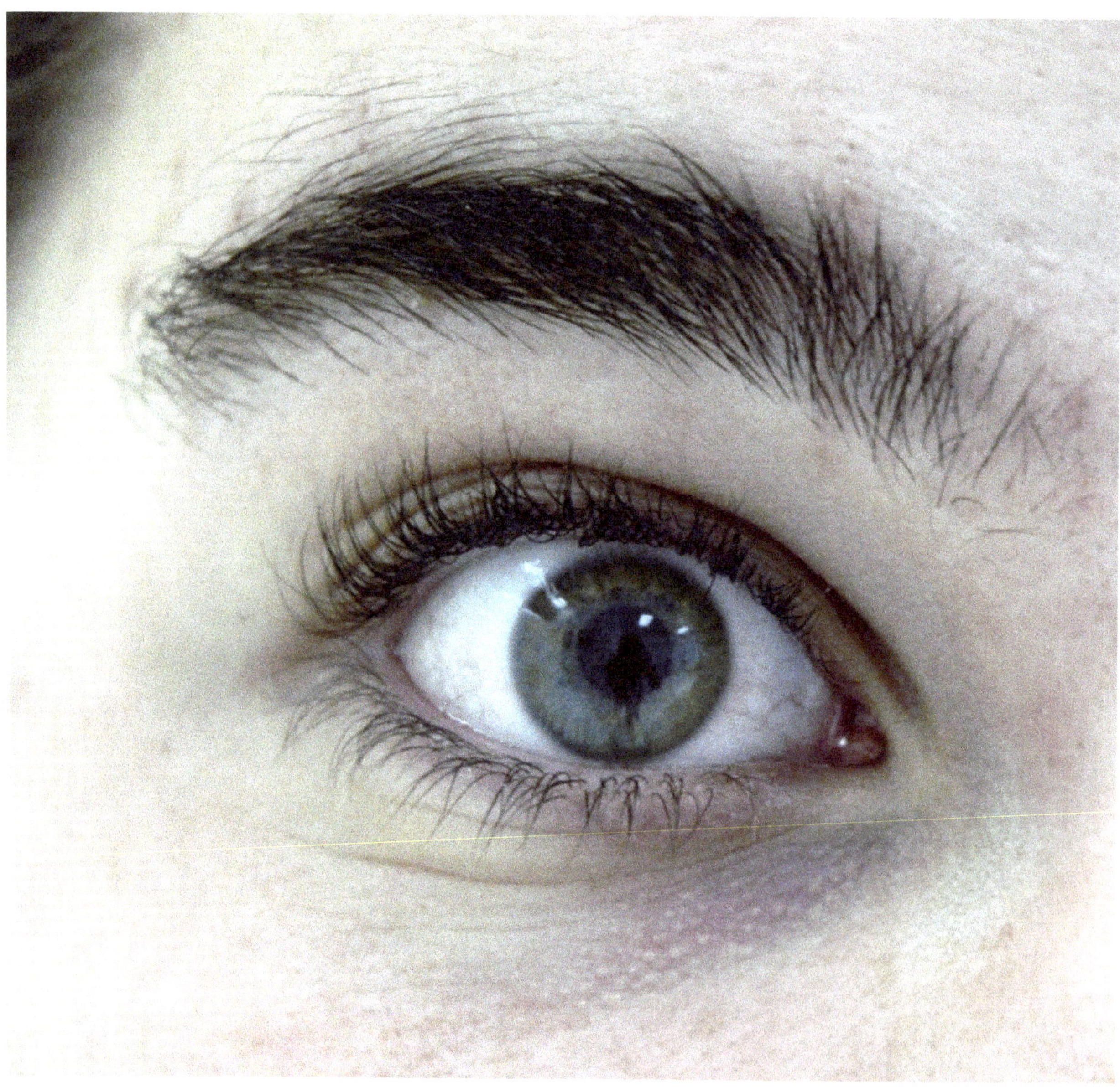

Now try drawing the surprised right eye yourself without the grid.

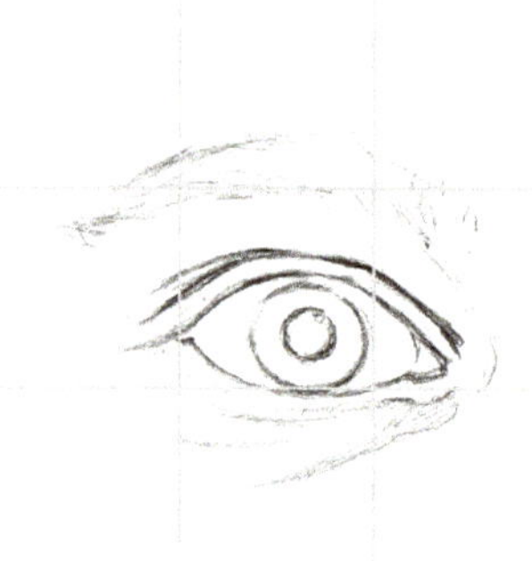

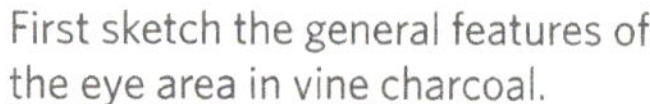

First sketch the general features of the eye area in vine charcoal.

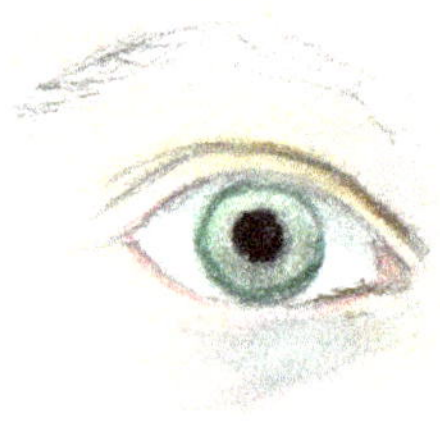

Block in the general areas of shadow, light and the iris using a light warm yellow for the skin tone and a light green for the iris.

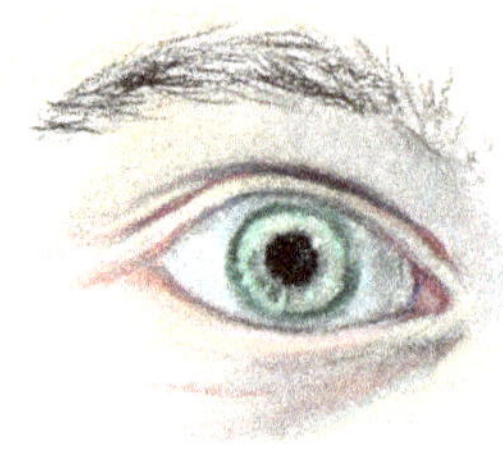

Identify the areas of light, shadow, and reflection light by layering on different light yellows, orange, light green, and pink to create rich skin tones.

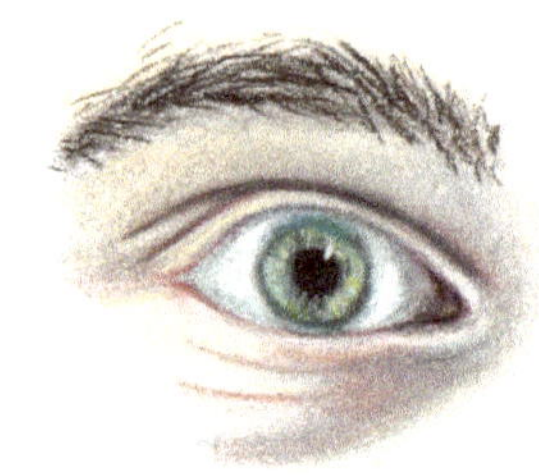

Continue to render the volume of the eye area, paying attention to how to eye sits within the eye socket and how the flesh sits around the eyeball. Continue to blend and add more pinks, greens and browns to create rich colors.

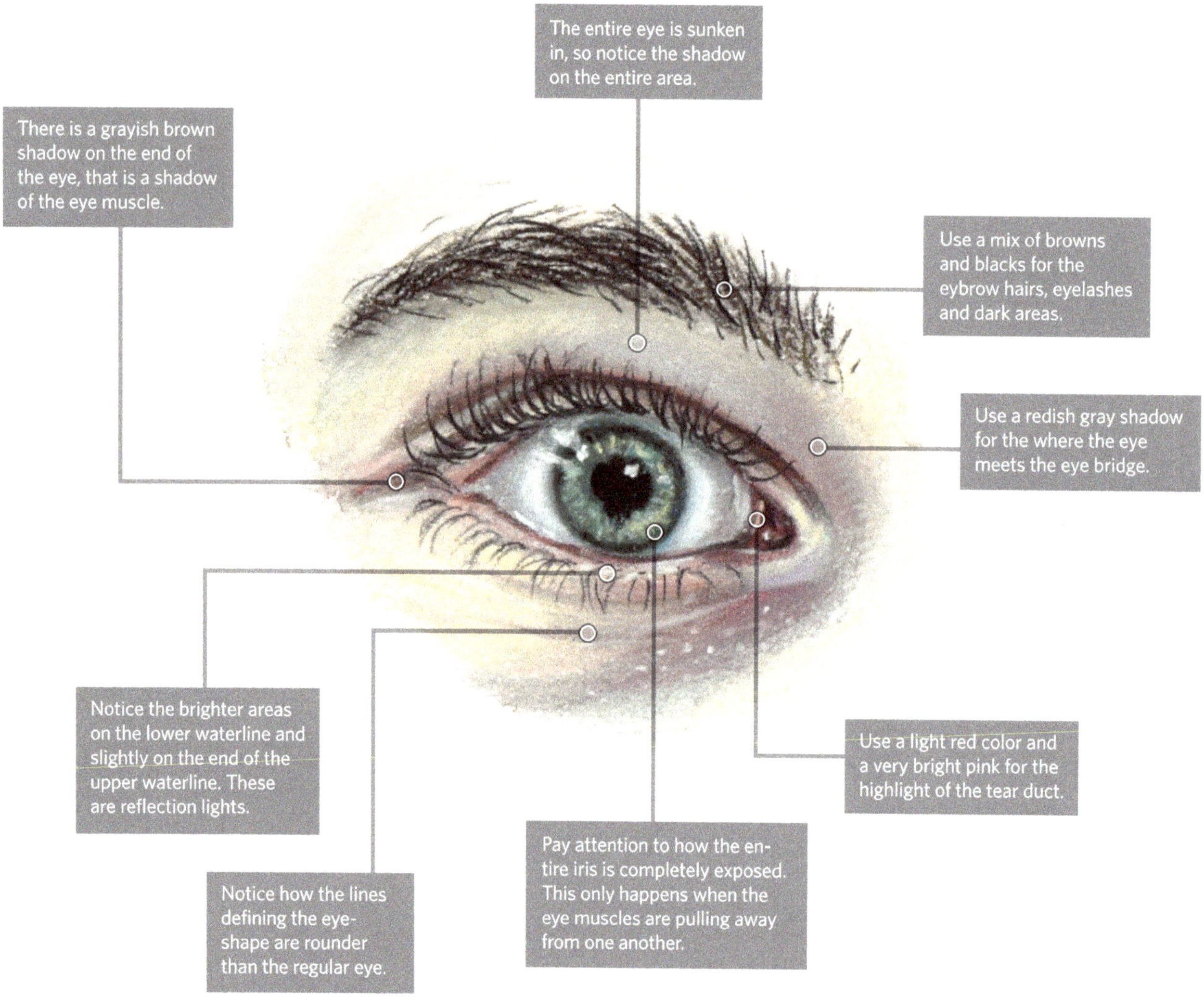

The entire eye is sunken in, so notice the shadow on the entire area.

There is a grayish brown shadow on the end of the eye, that is a shadow of the eye muscle.

Use a mix of browns and blacks for the eybrow hairs, eyelashes and dark areas.

Use a redish gray shadow for the where the eye meets the eye bridge.

Notice the brighter areas on the lower waterline and slightly on the end of the upper waterline. These are reflection lights.

Use a light red color and a very bright pink for the highlight of the tear duct.

Notice how the lines defining the eye-shape are rounder than the regular eye.

Pay attention to how the entire iris is completely exposed. This only happens when the eye muscles are pulling away from one another.

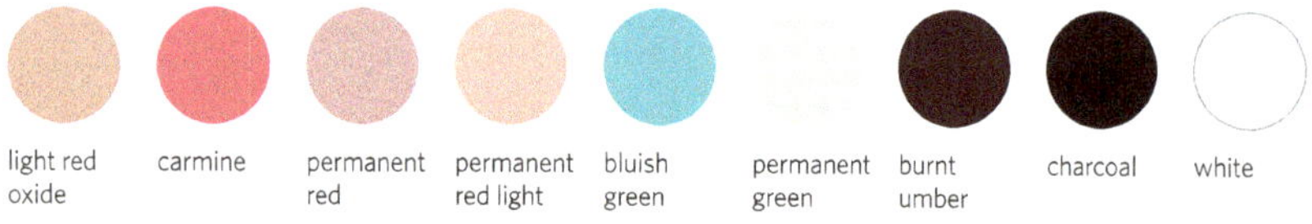

light red oxide, carmine, permanent red, permanent red light, bluish green, permanent green, burnt umber, charcoal, white

Now try drawing the surprised right eye yourself.

Now that you have practiced how to draw a surprised right eye in pastel following a step-by-step tutorial, use the page on the right to try and draw from life. You can draw from the picture below, use a mirror, or ask a friend to sit for you and try different variations of compositions.

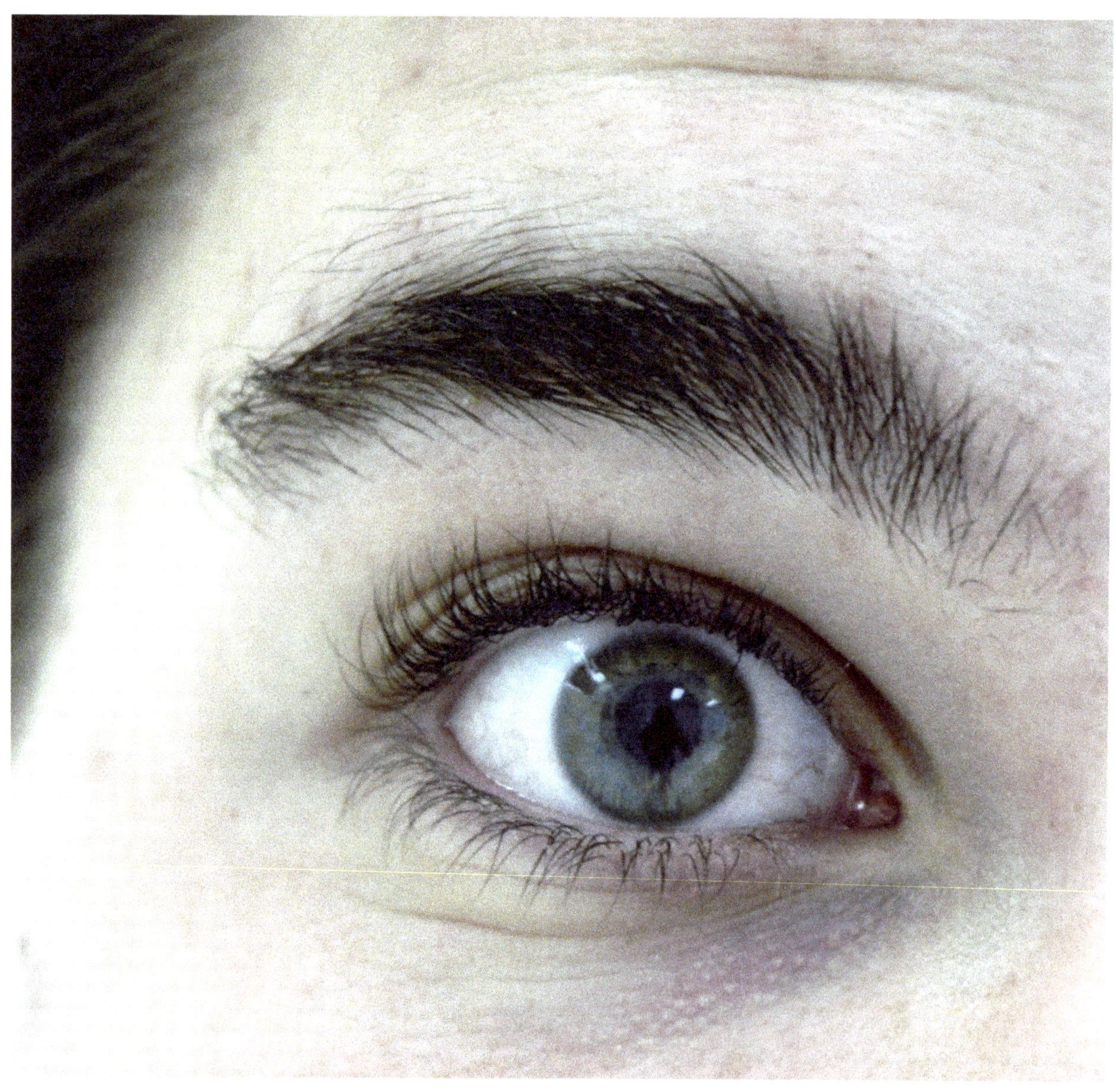

Now try drawing the surprised right eye yourself without the grid.

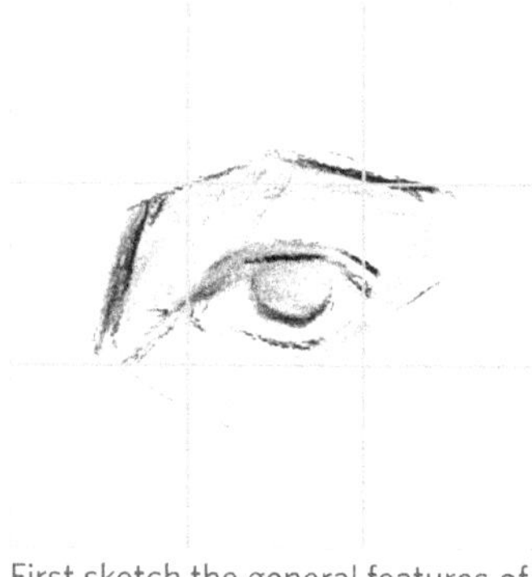

First sketch the general features of the eye area in vine charcoal.

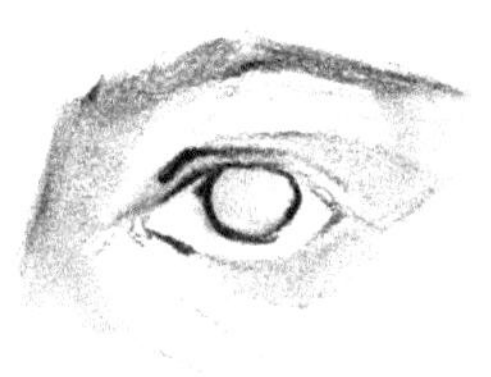

Block in the general areas of shadow, light and the iris.

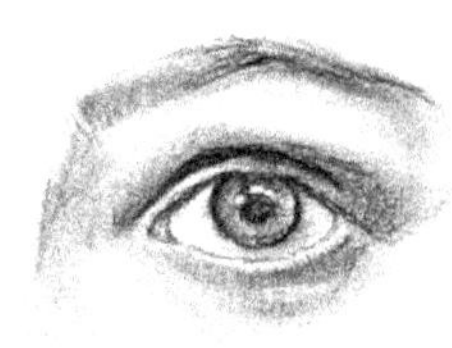

Identify the areas of light, shadow, and reflection light using smudging, shading, and erasing.

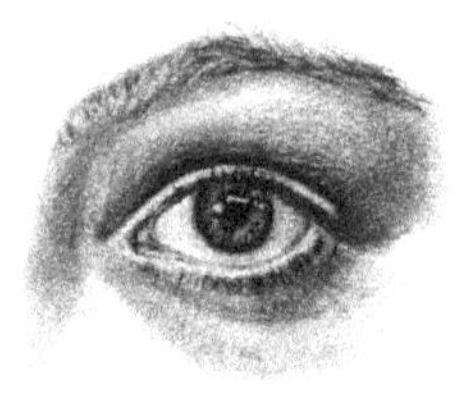

Continue to render the volume of the eye area, paying attention to how the eye sits within the eye socket and how the flesh sits around the eyeball.

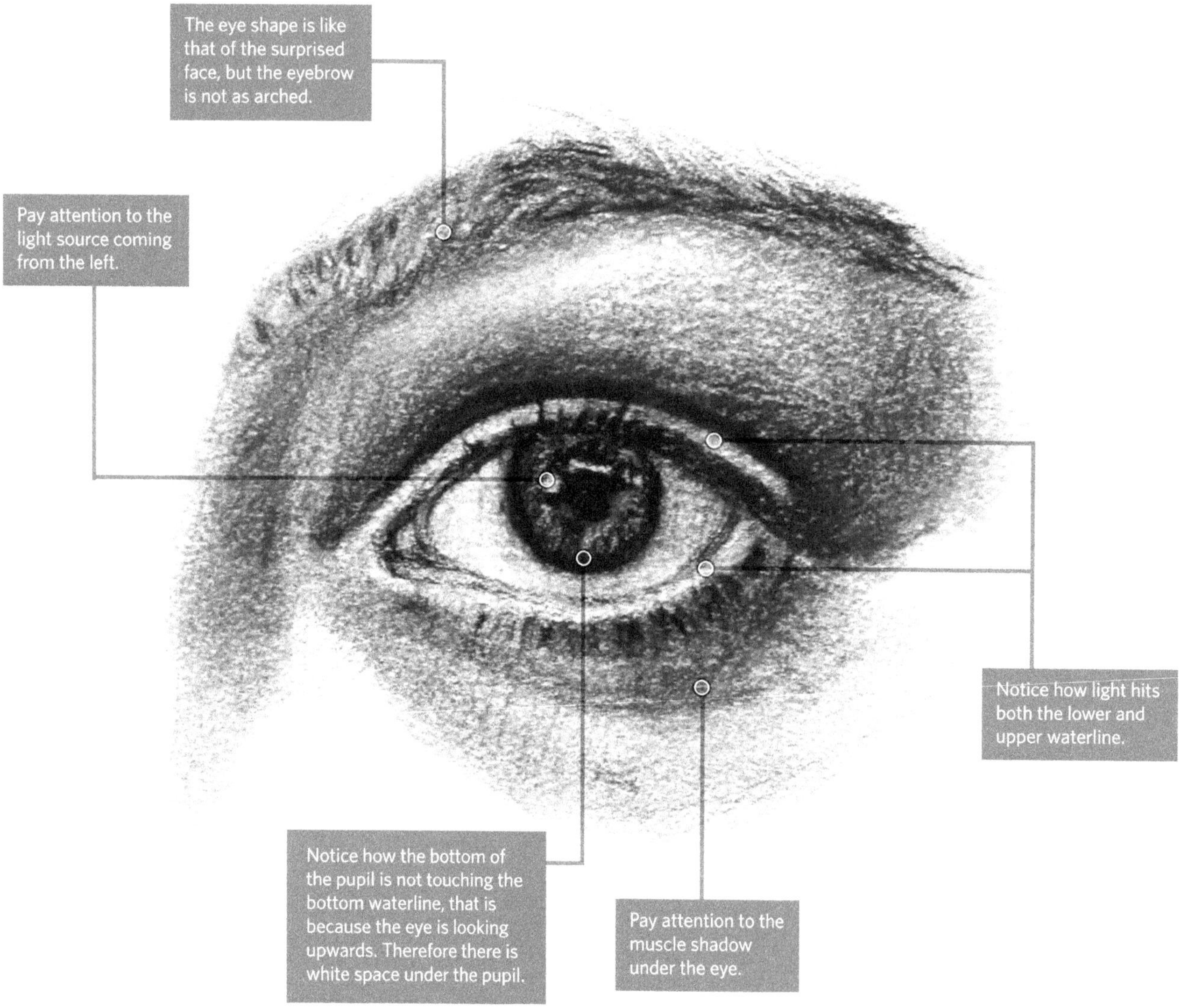

The eye shape is like that of the surprised face, but the eyebrow is not as arched.

Pay attention to the light source coming from the left.

Notice how light hits both the lower and upper waterline.

Notice how the bottom of the pupil is not touching the bottom waterline, that is because the eye is looking upwards. Therefore there is white space under the pupil.

Pay attention to the muscle shadow under the eye.

Now try drawing the upwards left eye yourself.

Now that you have practiced how to draw an upwards left eye in charcoal following a step-by-step tutorial, use the page on the right to try and draw from life. You can draw from the picture below, use a mirror, or ask a friend to sit for you and try different variations of compositions.

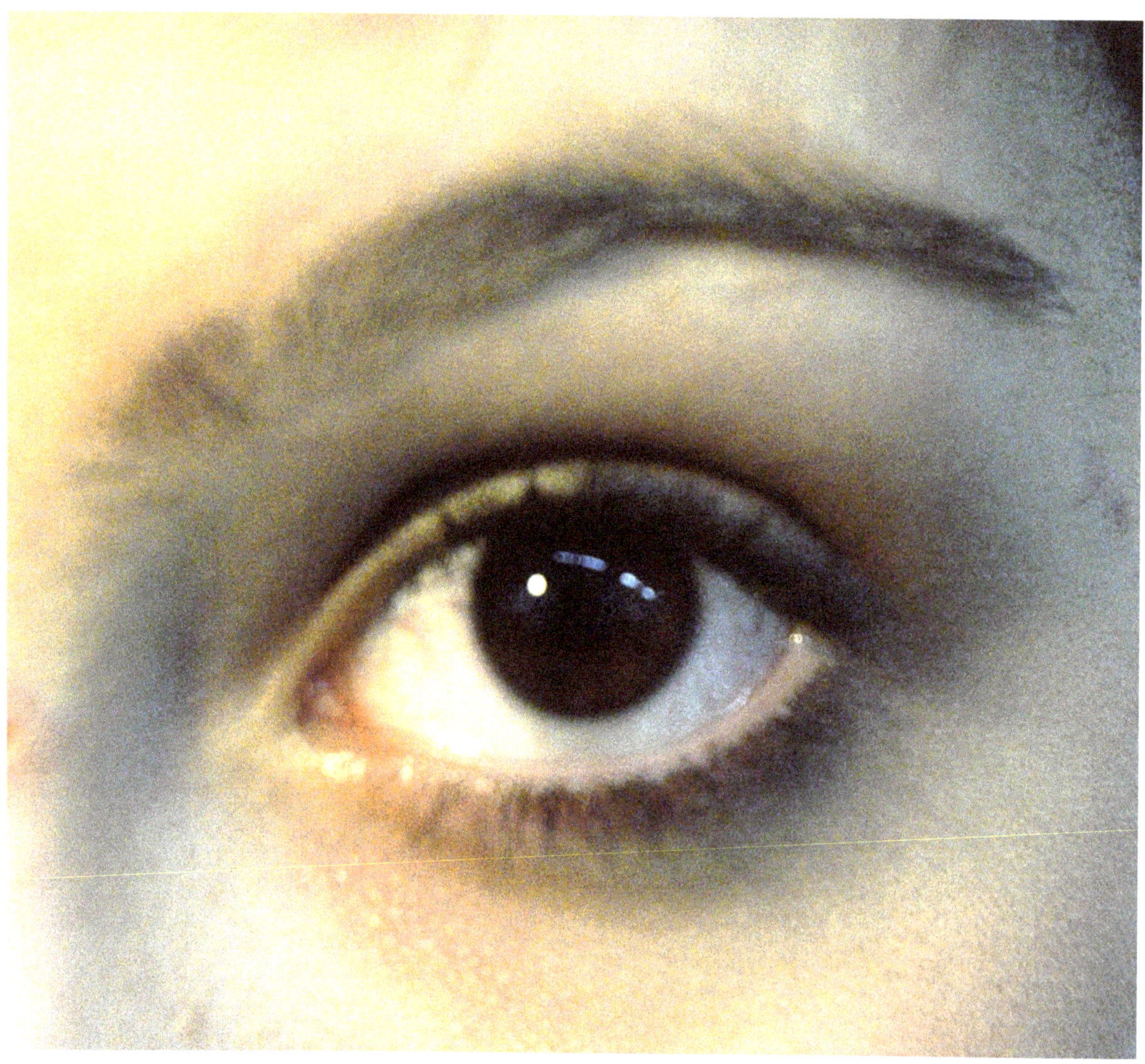

Now try drawing the upwards left eye yourself without the grid.

Now that you have practiced different ways the eyes can express emotion and how light and shadow affect the eyes, try a couple of other perspectives. Pay attention to the shape of the pupils in different perspectives, as well as the amount of white of the eyeball in each position, the pupil isn't always a perfect circle. Because of the muscle above the eye, the shape of the eyebrow changes as well.

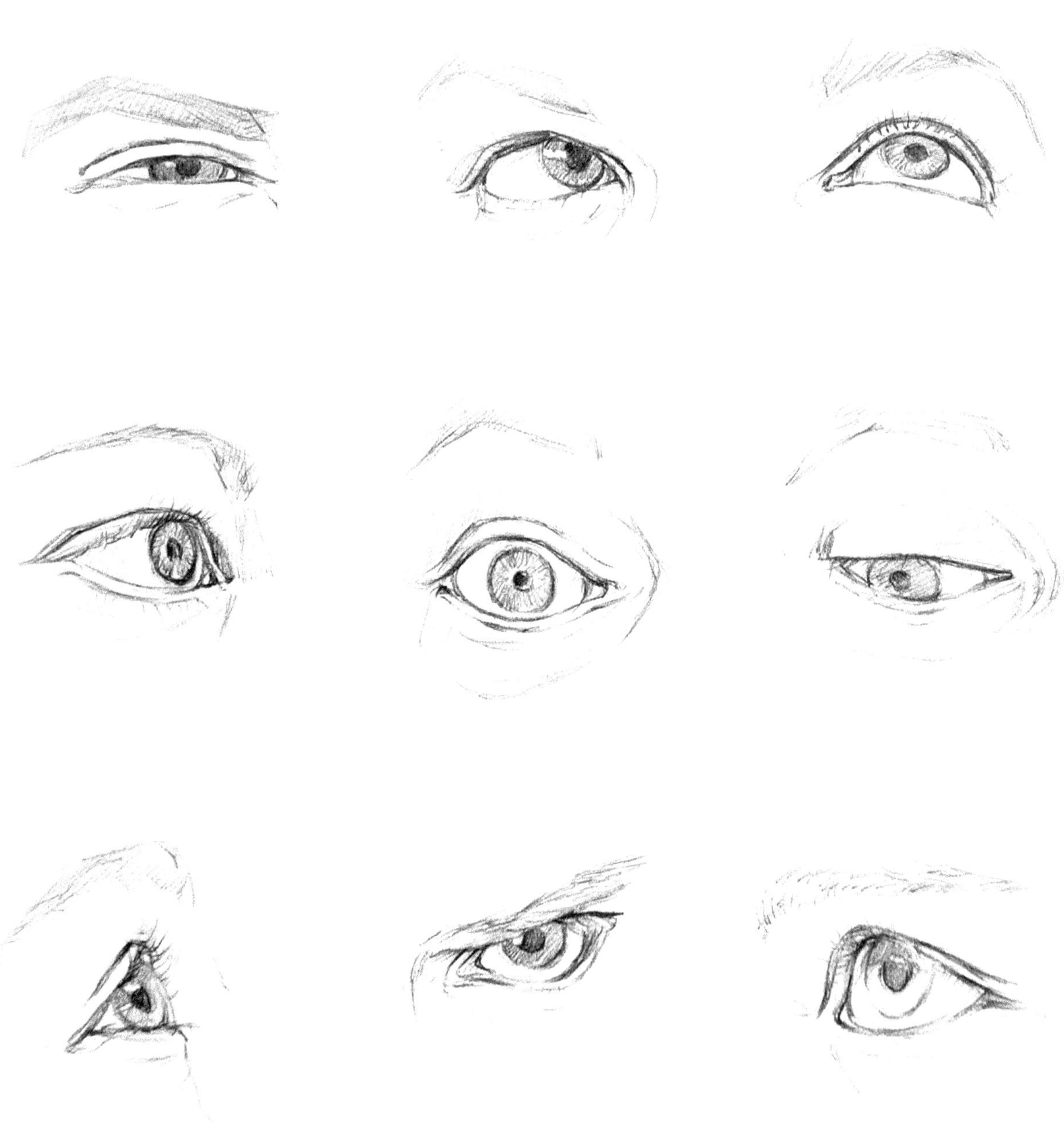

Now try drawing the basic eye perspectives yourself.

Drawing the nose can be difficult as there are few hard lines to help define its structure. To help, it is best to divide it into simple flat planes. The plane that forms the bridge of the nose will receive the most highlight. The area least in shadow is the plane that holds the nostrils. Once you have these areas blocked in, you can easily add more details and soften the planes.

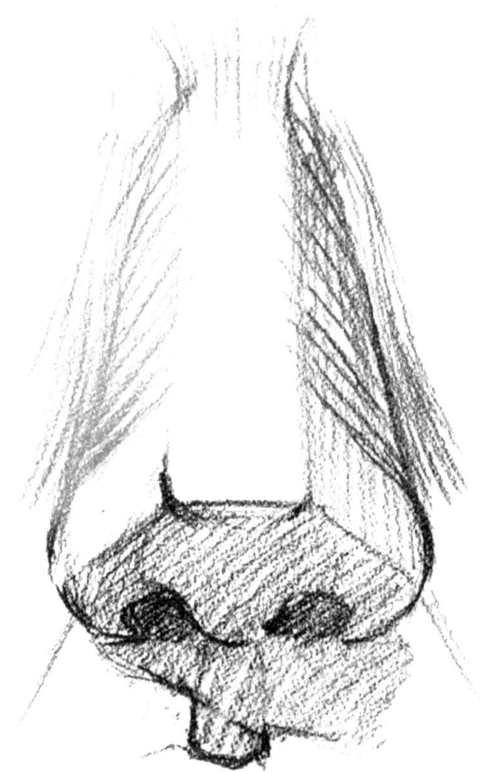

Now try drawing the basic nose structure yourself.

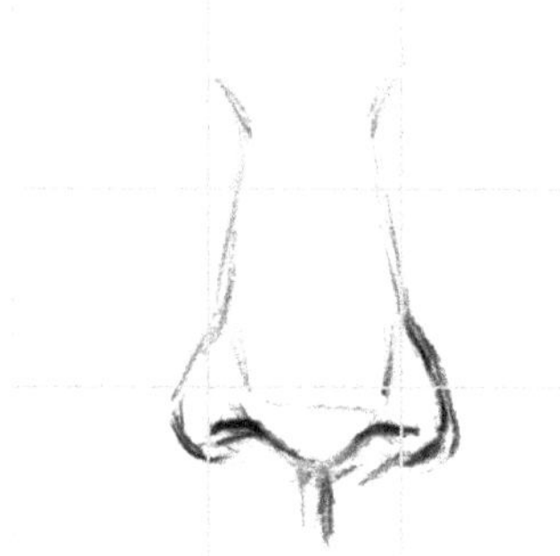

First sketch the general features of the nose area in vine charcoal.

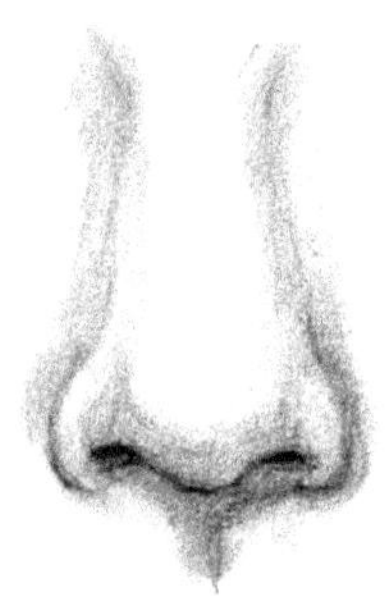

Block in the general areas of shadow and light.

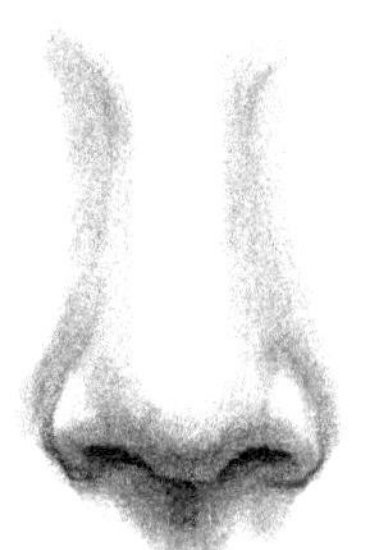

Identify the areas of light, shadow, and reflection light using smudging, shading, and erasing.

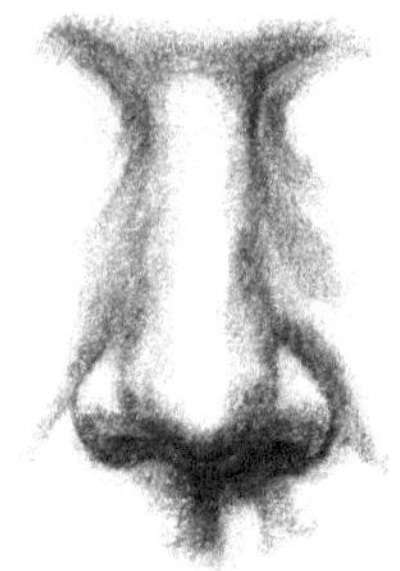

Continue to render the volume of the nose area, paying attention to the gradients describing the volume of the nose.

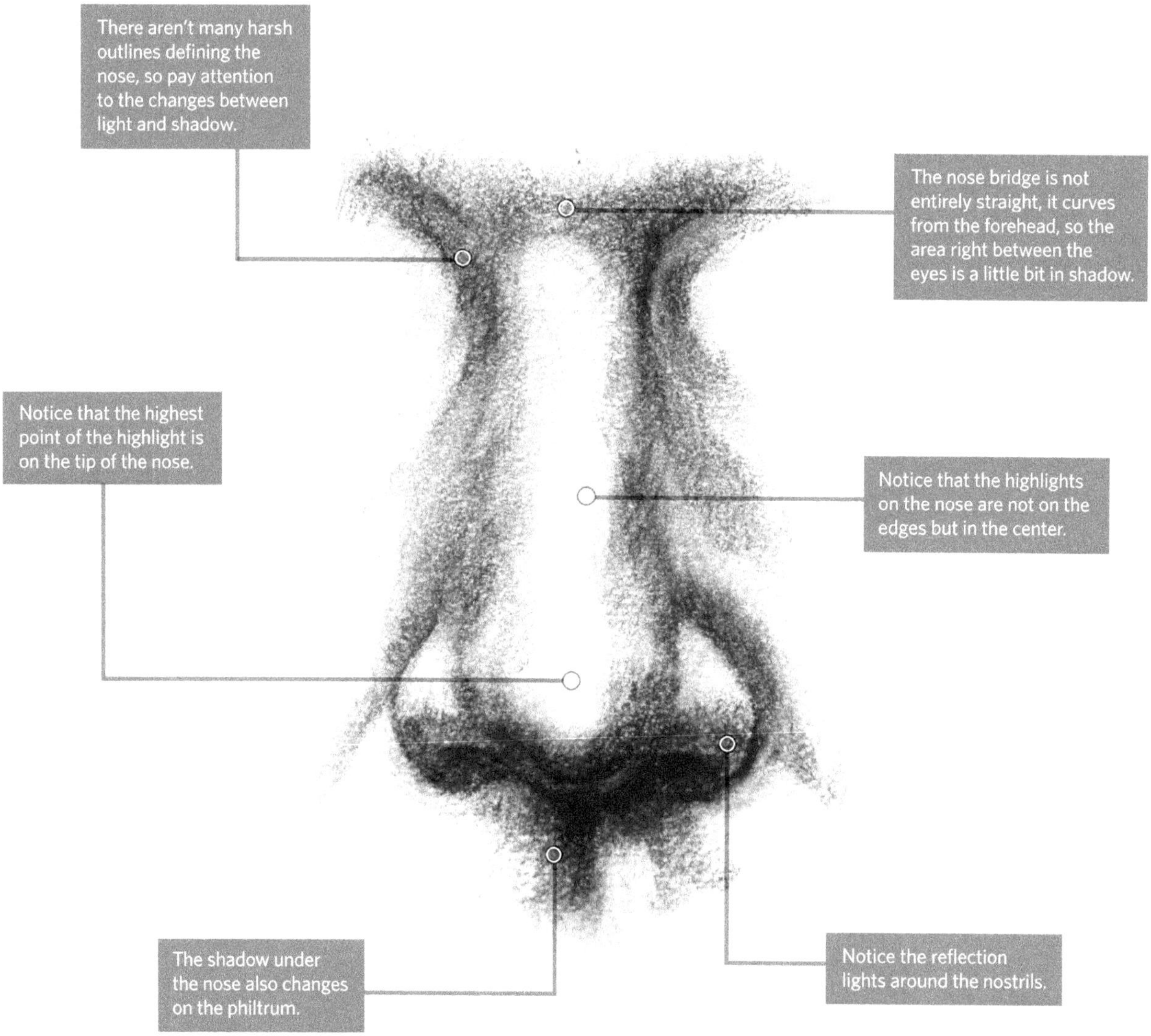

There aren't many harsh outlines defining the nose, so pay attention to the changes between light and shadow.

The nose bridge is not entirely straight, it curves from the forehead, so the area right between the eyes is a little bit in shadow.

Notice that the highest point of the highlight is on the tip of the nose.

Notice that the highlights on the nose are not on the edges but in the center.

The shadow under the nose also changes on the philtrum.

Notice the reflection lights around the nostrils.

Now try drawing the front side of the nose yourself.

Now that you have practiced how to draw the front of the nose in charcoal following a step-by-step tutorial, use the page on the right to try and draw from life. You can draw from the picture below, use a mirror, or ask a friend to sit for you and try different variations of compositions.

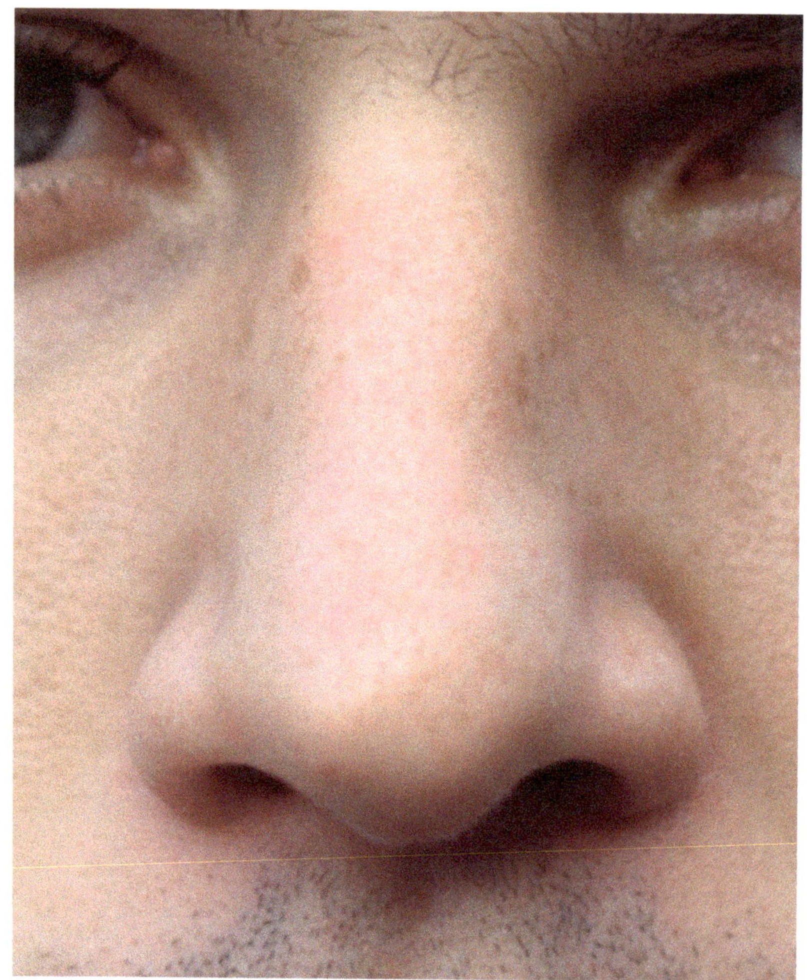

Now try drawing the front side of the nose yourself without the grid.

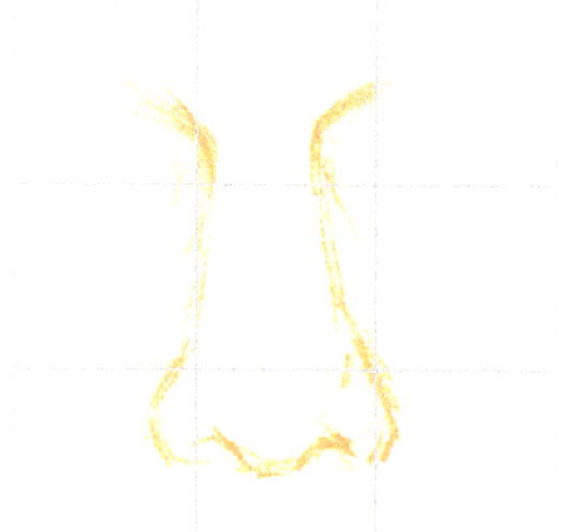

First sketch the general features of the nose area in yellow ochre.

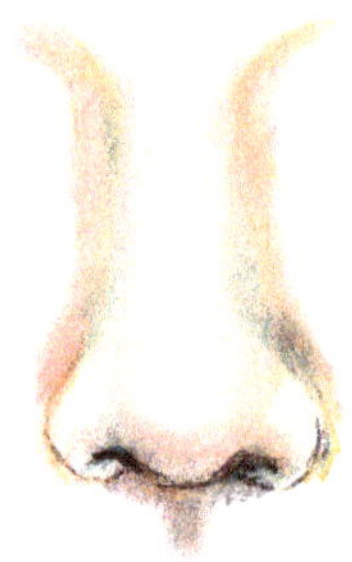

Block in the general areas of shadow and light using pinks, oranges, and a few greens.

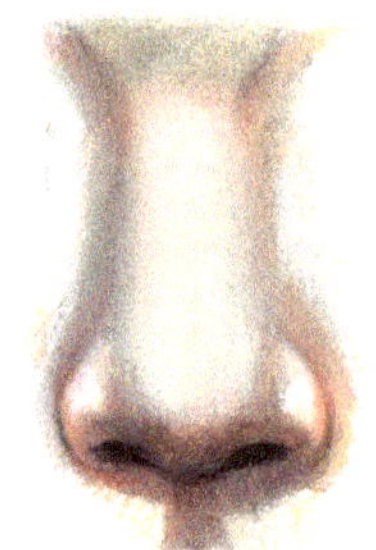

Identify the areas of light, shadow, and reflection light by layering on different skin tone colors, browns, oranges, peach, pinks, yellow, and a little bit of greens and blues.

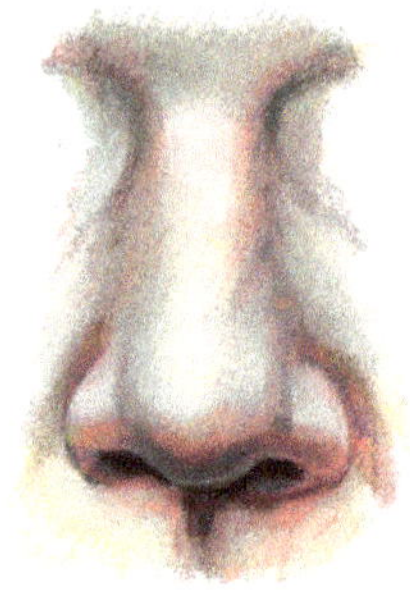

Continue to render the volume of the nose area, paying attention the areas of subtle gradient shifts to render the volume of the nose. Add greens and blues to make the skin tones more rich.

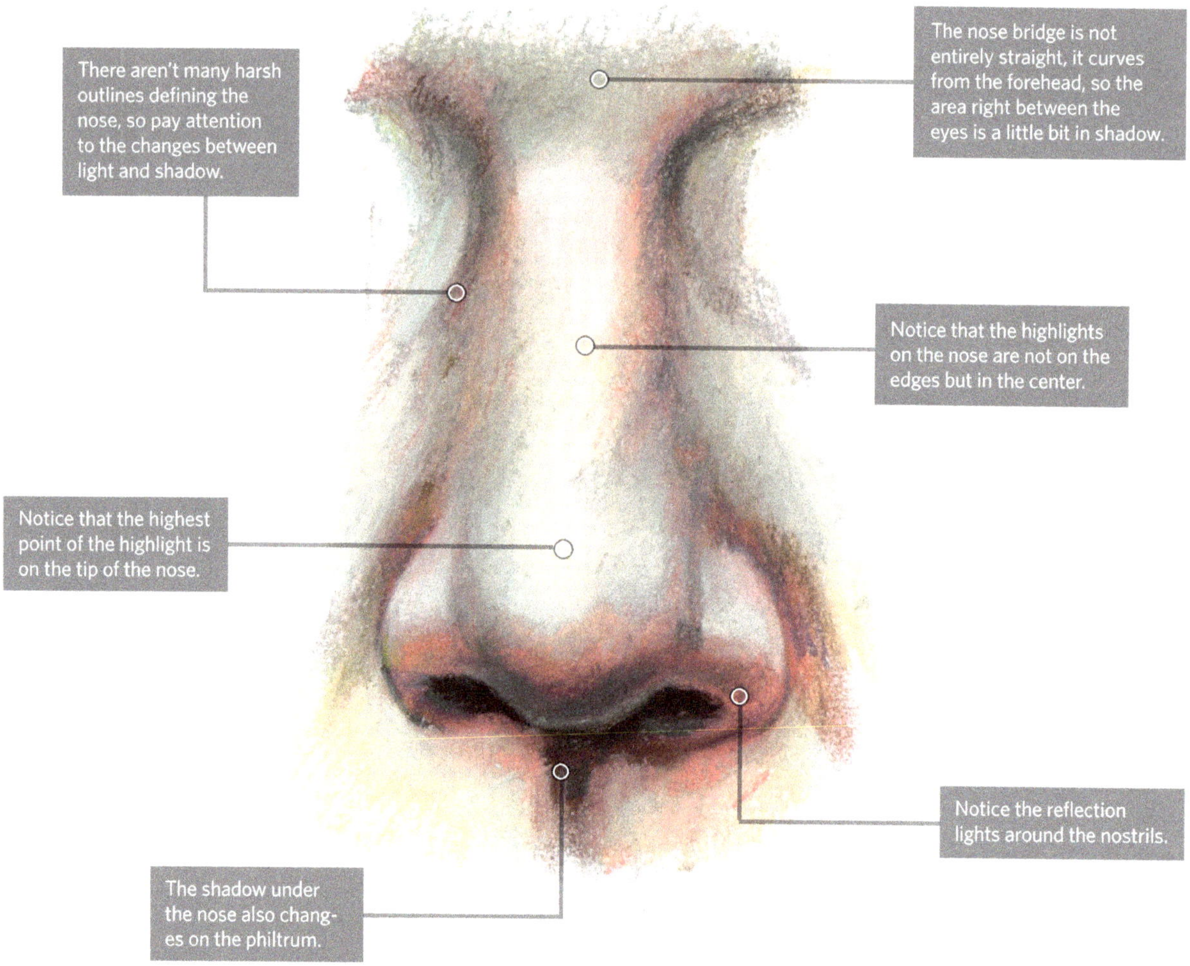

There aren't many harsh outlines defining the nose, so pay attention to the changes between light and shadow.

The nose bridge is not entirely straight, it curves from the forehead, so the area right between the eyes is a little bit in shadow.

Notice that the highlights on the nose are not on the edges but in the center.

Notice that the highest point of the highlight is on the tip of the nose.

Notice the reflection lights around the nostrils.

The shadow under the nose also changes on the philtrum.

light red oxide

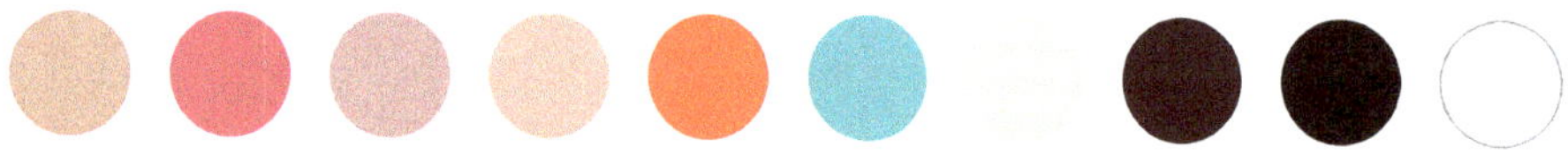

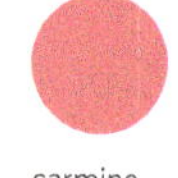
carmine

permanent red

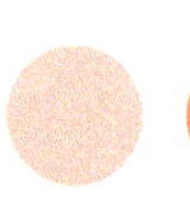
permanent red light

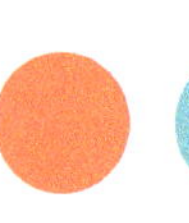
cadmium orange

bluish green

permanent green

burnt umber

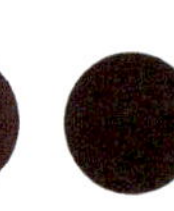
charcoal

white

Now try drawing the front side of the nose yourself.

Now that you have practiced how to draw the front of the nose in pastel following a step-by-step tutorial, use the page on the right to try and draw from life. You can draw from the picture below, use a mirror, or ask a friend to sit for you and try different variations of compositions.

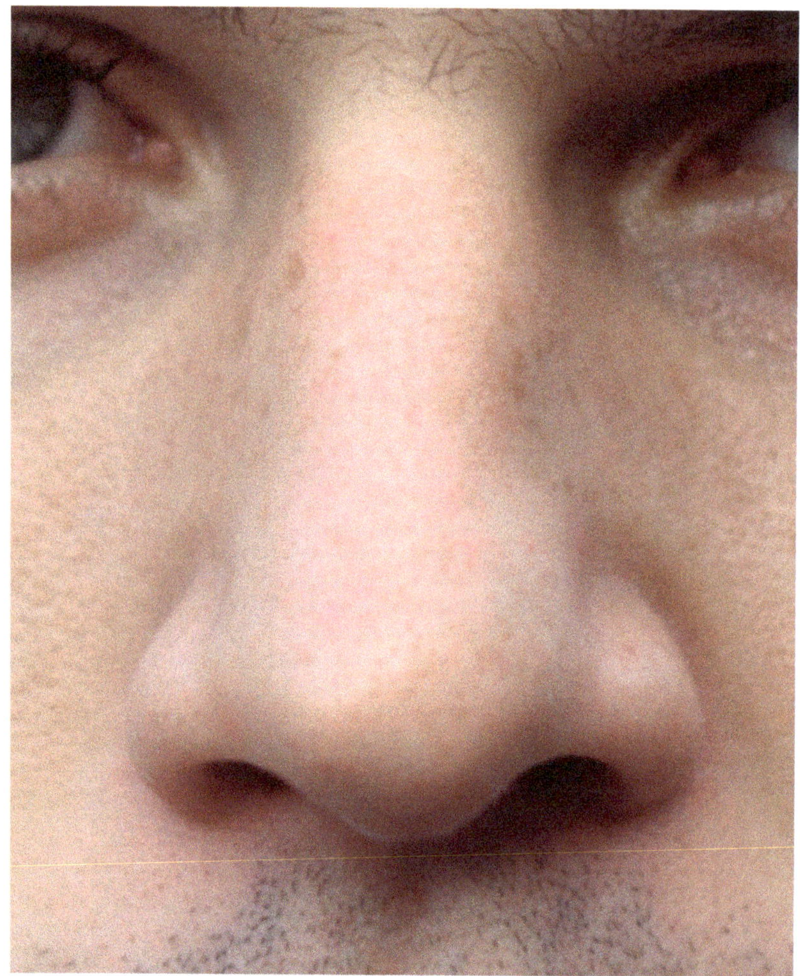

Now try drawing the front side of the nose yourself without the grid.

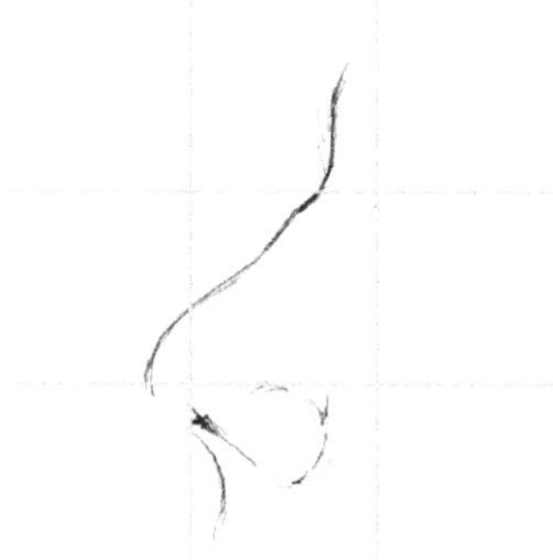
First sketch the general features of the nose area in vine charcoal.

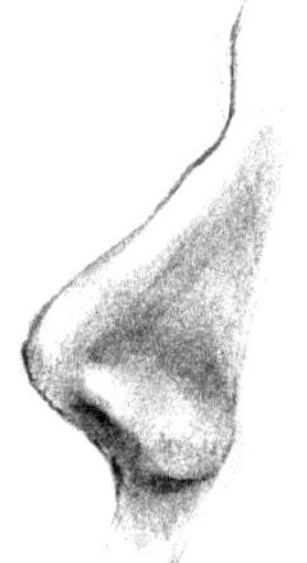
Block in the general areas of shadow and light

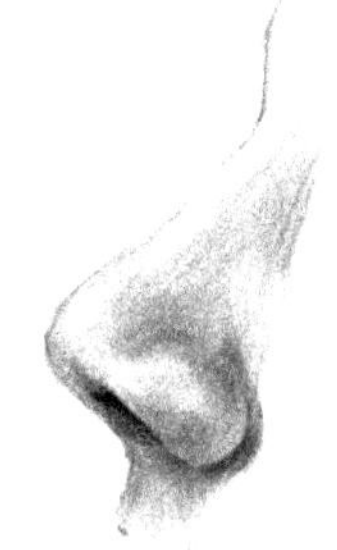
Identify the areas of light, shadow, and reflection light using smudging, shading, and erasing.

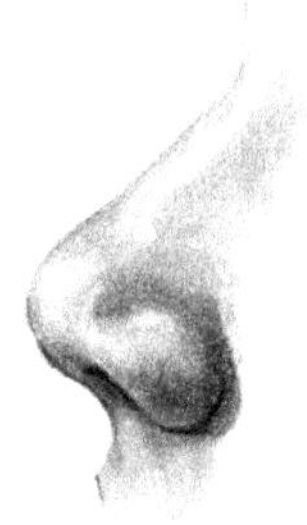
Continue to render the volume of the nose area, paying attention to the gradients describing the volume of the nose.

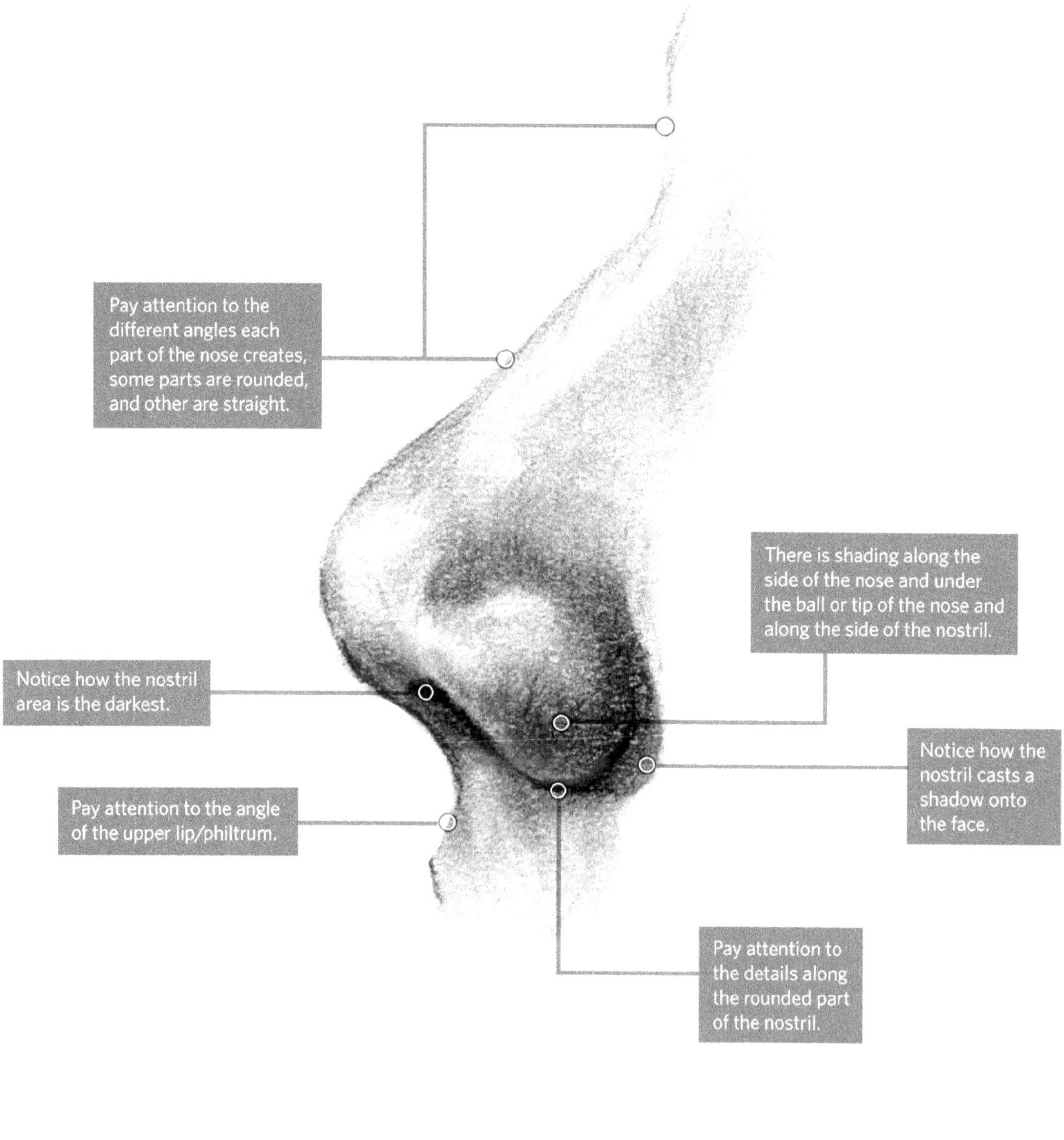

Pay attention to the different angles each part of the nose creates, some parts are rounded, and other are straight.

There is shading along the side of the nose and under the ball or tip of the nose and along the side of the nostril.

Notice how the nostril area is the darkest.

Notice how the nostril casts a shadow onto the face.

Pay attention to the angle of the upper lip/philtrum.

Pay attention to the details along the rounded part of the nostril.

Now try drawing the left side of the nose yourself.

Now that you have practiced how to draw the left side of the nose in charcoal following a step-by-step tutorial, use the page on the right to try and draw from life. You can draw from the picture below, use a mirror, or ask a friend to sit for you and try different variations of compositions.

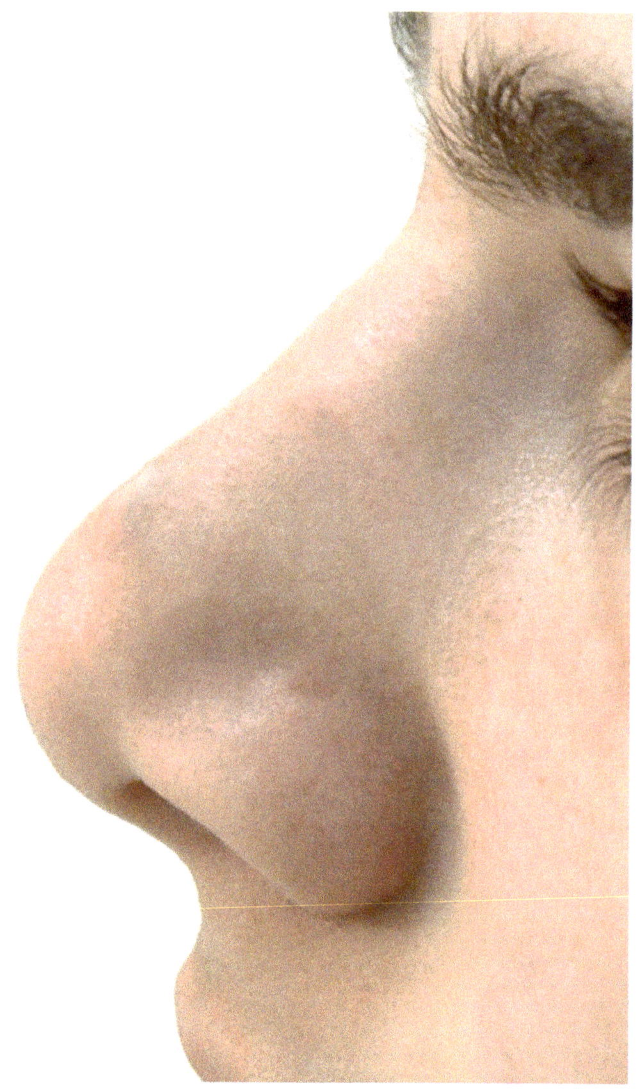

Now try drawing the left side of the nose yourself without the grid.

NOSE (LEFT SIDE) IN PASTEL: TIPS

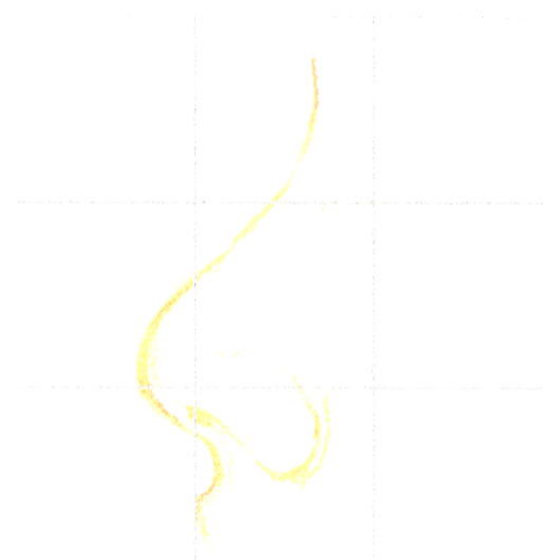

First sketch the general features of the nose area in yellow ochre.

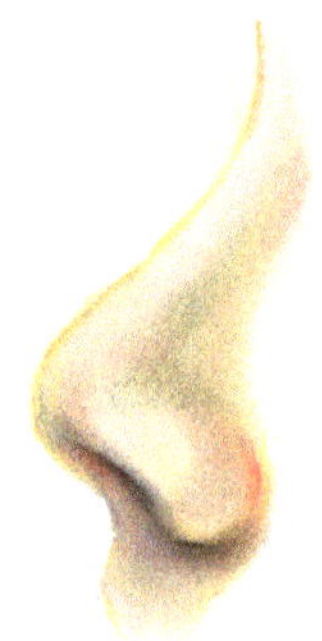

Block in the general areas of shadow and light using pinks, oranges, and a few greens.

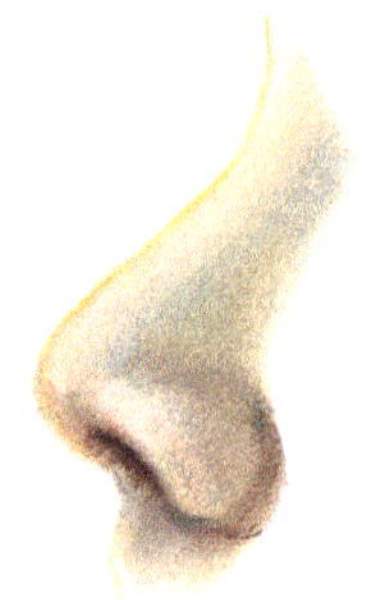

Identify the areas of light, shadow, and reflection light by layering on different skin tone colors, browns, oranges, peach, pinks, yellow, and a few greens and blues.

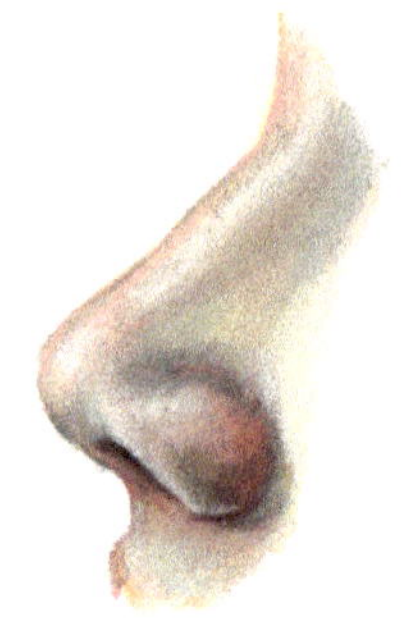

Continue to render the volume of the nose area, paying attention the areas of subtle gradient shifts to render the volume of the nose. Add greens and blues to make the skin tones more rich.

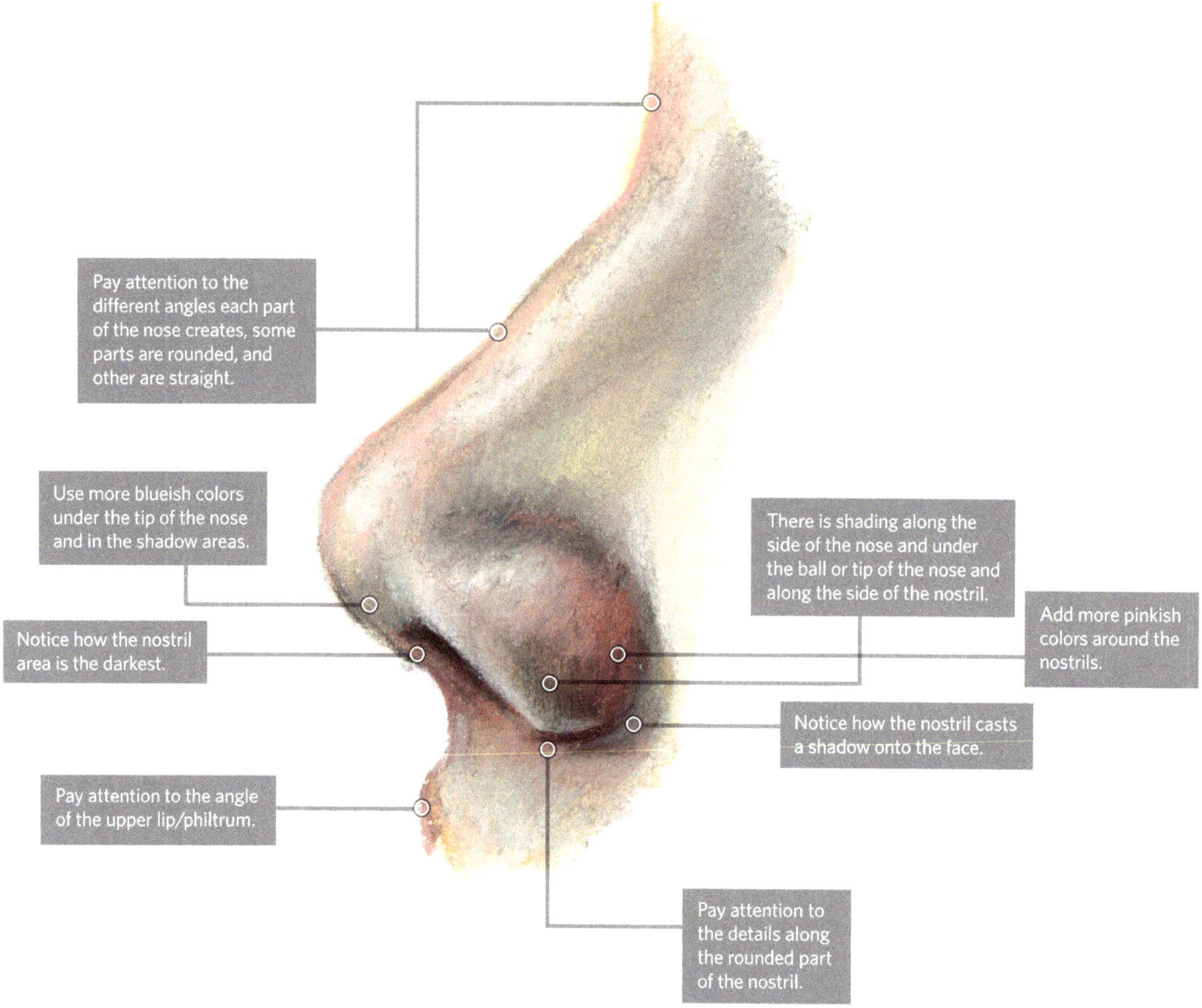

Pay attention to the different angles each part of the nose creates, some parts are rounded, and other are straight.

Use more blueish colors under the tip of the nose and in the shadow areas.

Notice how the nostril area is the darkest.

Pay attention to the angle of the upper lip/philtrum.

There is shading along the side of the nose and under the ball or tip of the nose and along the side of the nostril.

Add more pinkish colors around the nostrils.

Notice how the nostril casts a shadow onto the face.

Pay attention to the details along the rounded part of the nostril.

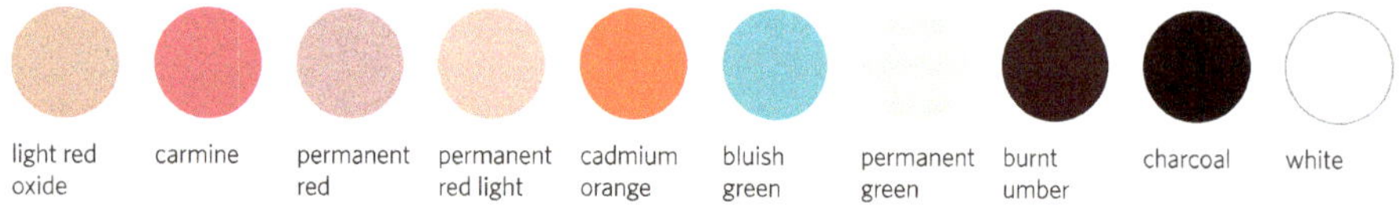

light red oxide | carmine | permanent red | permanent red light | cadmium orange | bluish green | permanent green | burnt umber | charcoal | white

Now try drawing the left side of the nose yourself.

Now that you have practiced how to draw the left side of the nose in pastel following a step-by-step tutorial, use the page on the right to try and draw from life. You can draw from the picture below, use a mirror, or ask a friend to sit for you and try different variations of compositions.

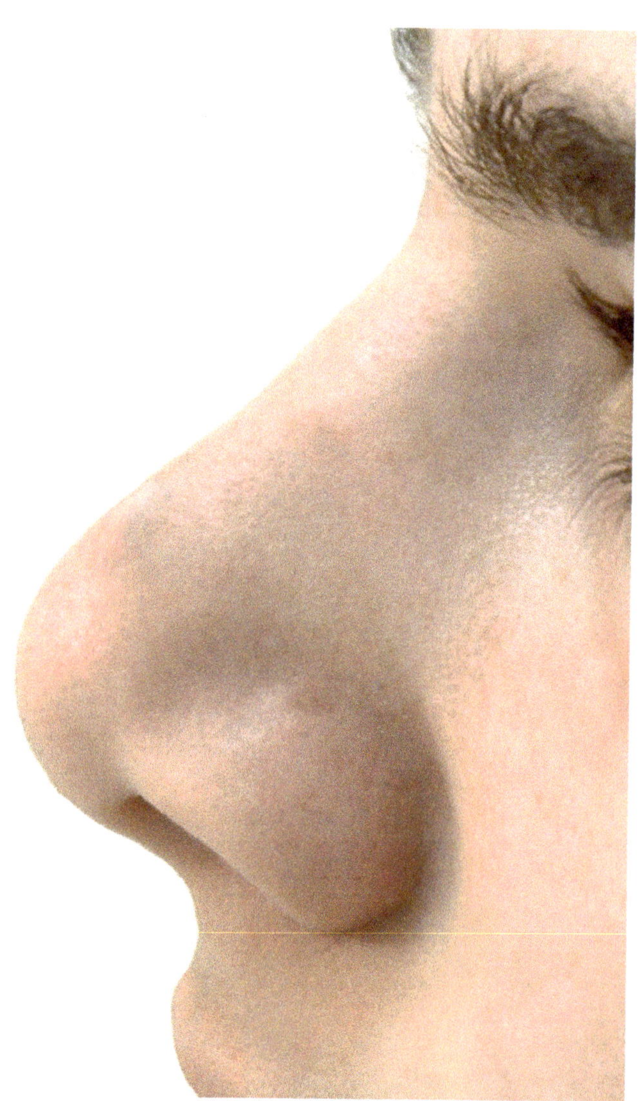

Now try drawing the left side of the nose yourself without the grid.

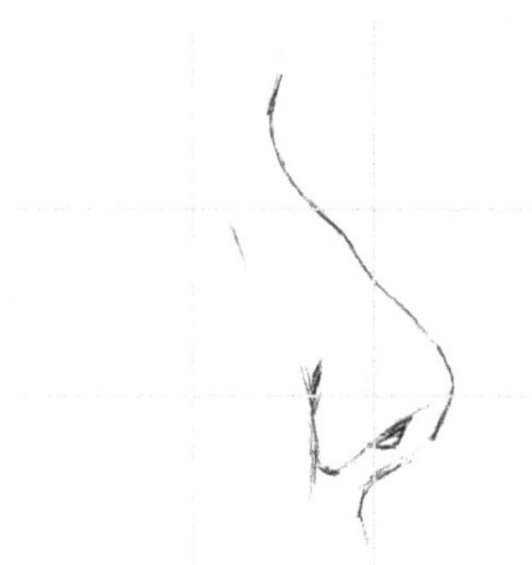

First sketch the general features of the nose area in vine charcoal.

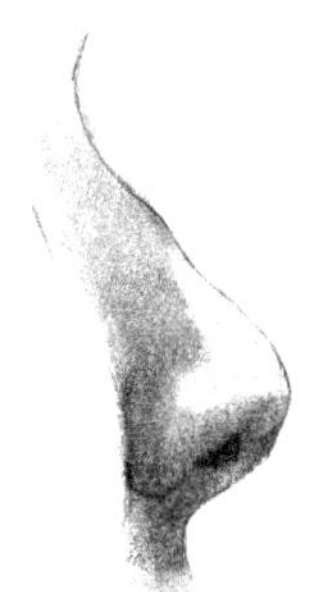

Block in the general areas of shadow and light.

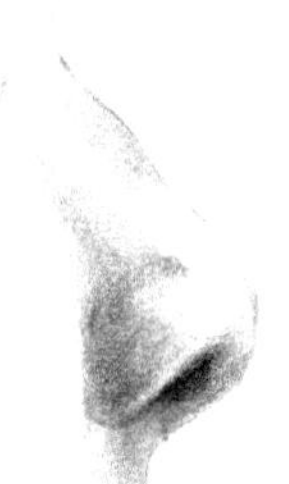

Identify the areas of light, shadow, and reflection light using smudging, shading, and erasing.

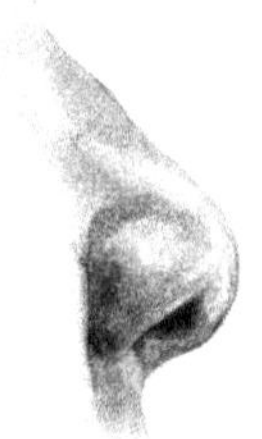

Continue to render the volume of the nose area, paying attention to the gradients describing the volume of the nose.

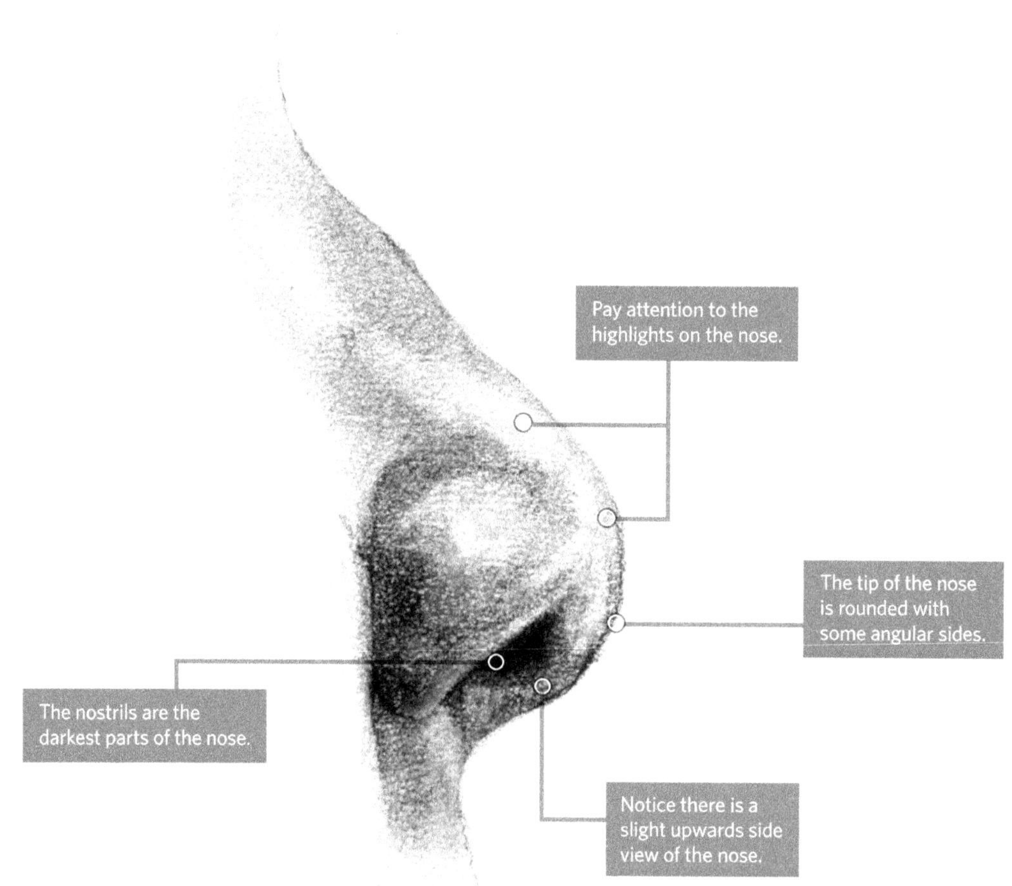

Now try drawing the right side of the nose yourself.

Now that you have practiced how to draw the right side of the nose in charcoal following a step-by-step tutorial, use the page on the right to try and draw from life. You can draw from the picture below, use a mirror, or ask a friend to sit for you and try different variations of compositions.

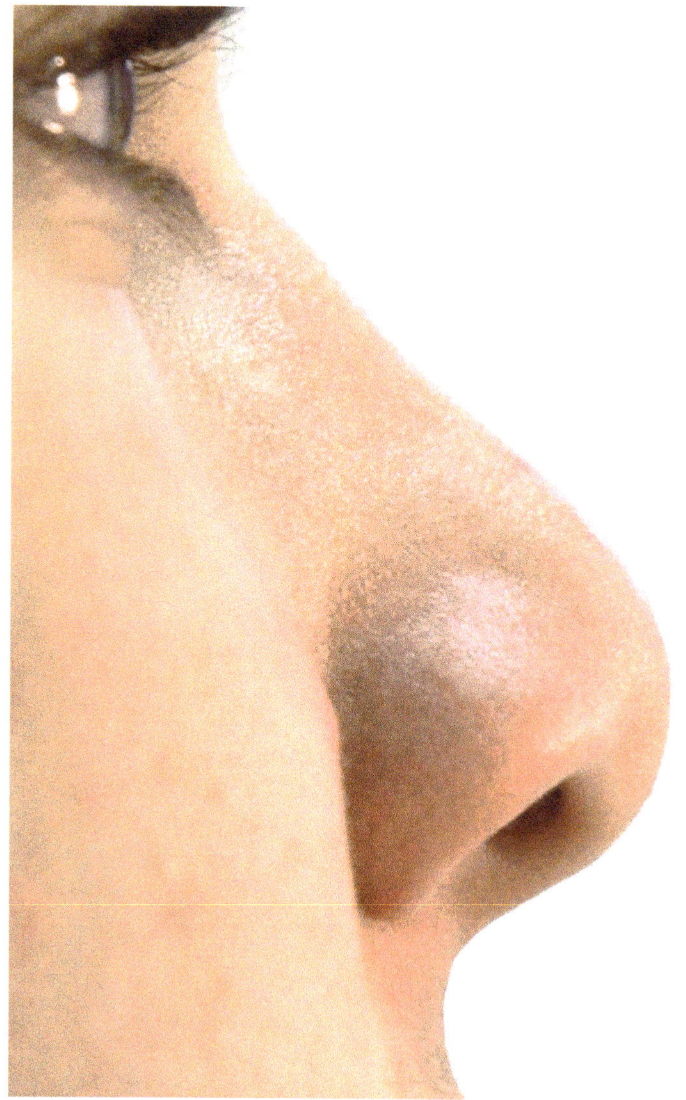

Now try drawing the right side of the nose yourself without the grid.

First sketch the general features of the nose area in yellow ochre.

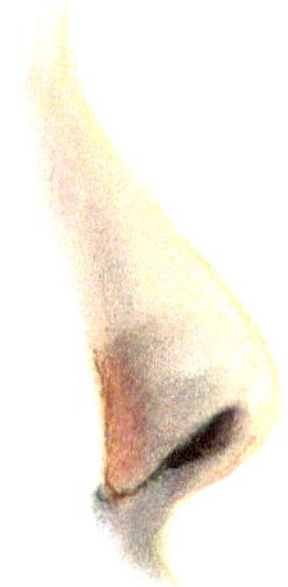

Block in the general areas of shadow and light using pinks, oranges, burnt sienna, and a few greens.

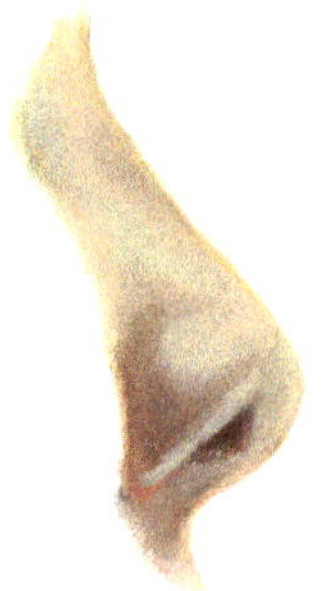

Identify the areas of light, shadow, and reflection light by layering on different skin tone colors, browns, oranges, peach, pinks, yellow, and a few greens and blues.

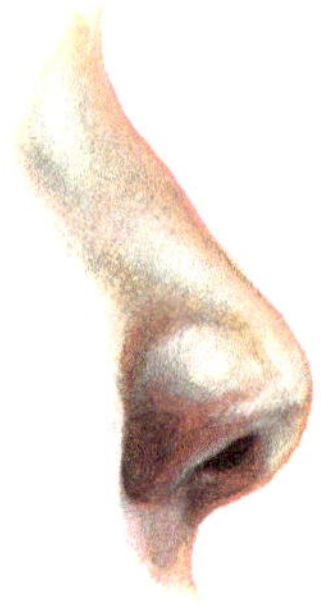

Continue to render the volume of the nose area, paying attention the areas of subtle gradient shifts to render the volume of the nose. Add greens and blues to make the skin tones more rich.

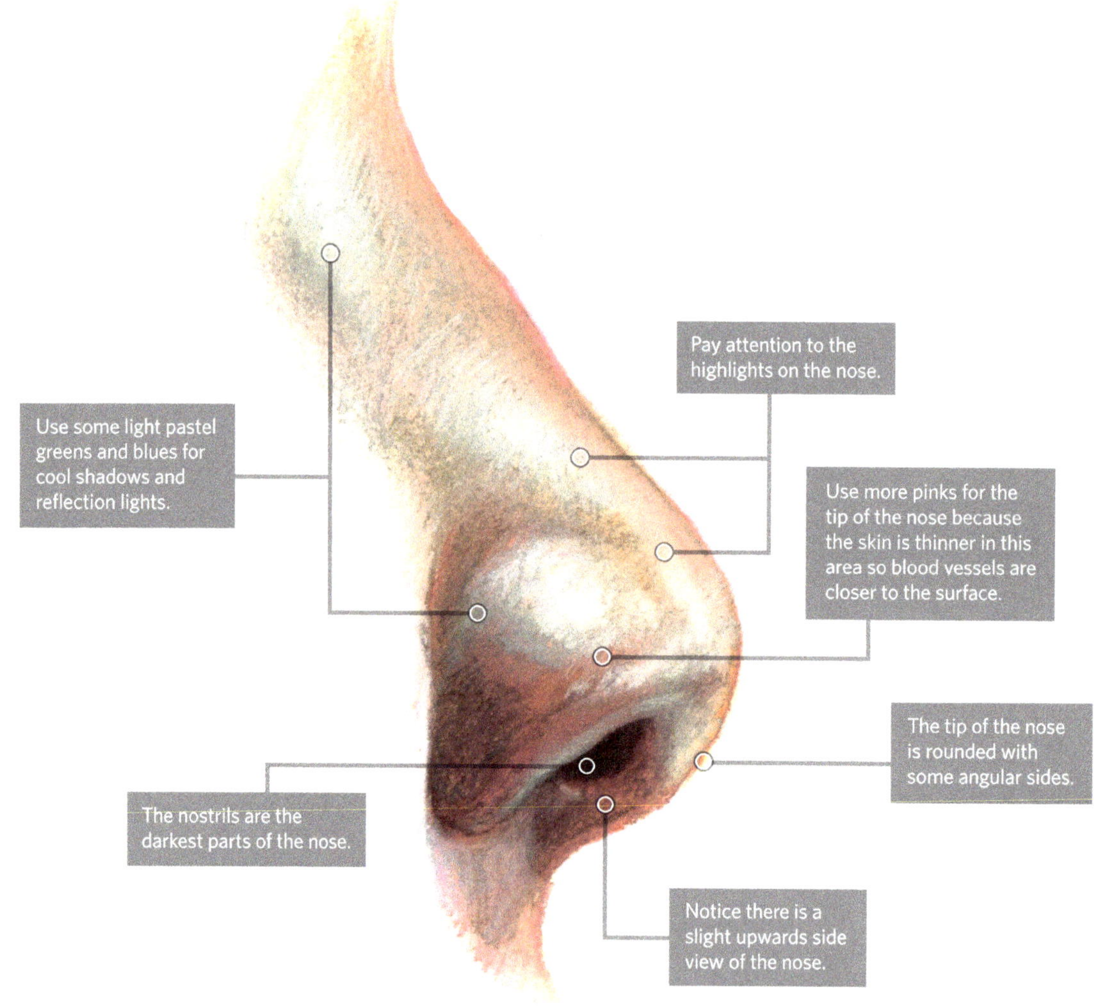

light red oxide

carmine

permanent red

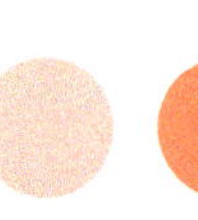
permanent red light

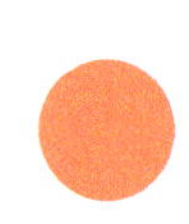
cadmium orange

bluish green

permanent green

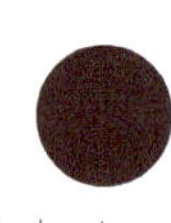
burnt umber

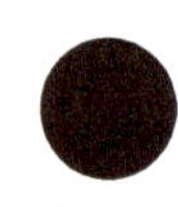
charcoal

white

Now try drawing the right side of the nose yourself.

Now that you have practiced how to draw the right side of the nose in pastel following a step-by-step tutorial, use the page on the right to try and draw from life. You can draw from the picture below, use a mirror, or ask a friend to sit for you and try different variations of compositions.

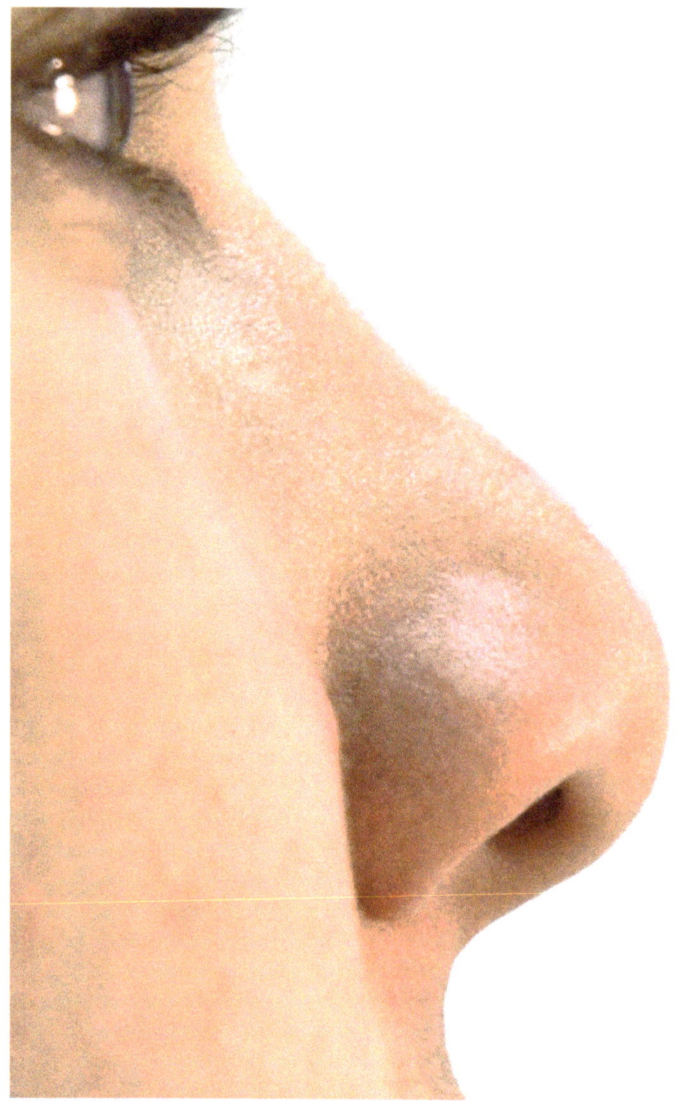

Now try drawing the right side of the nose yourself without the grid.

Pay attention to the different angles of the face and how it affects the position of the eyes, nose and mouth.

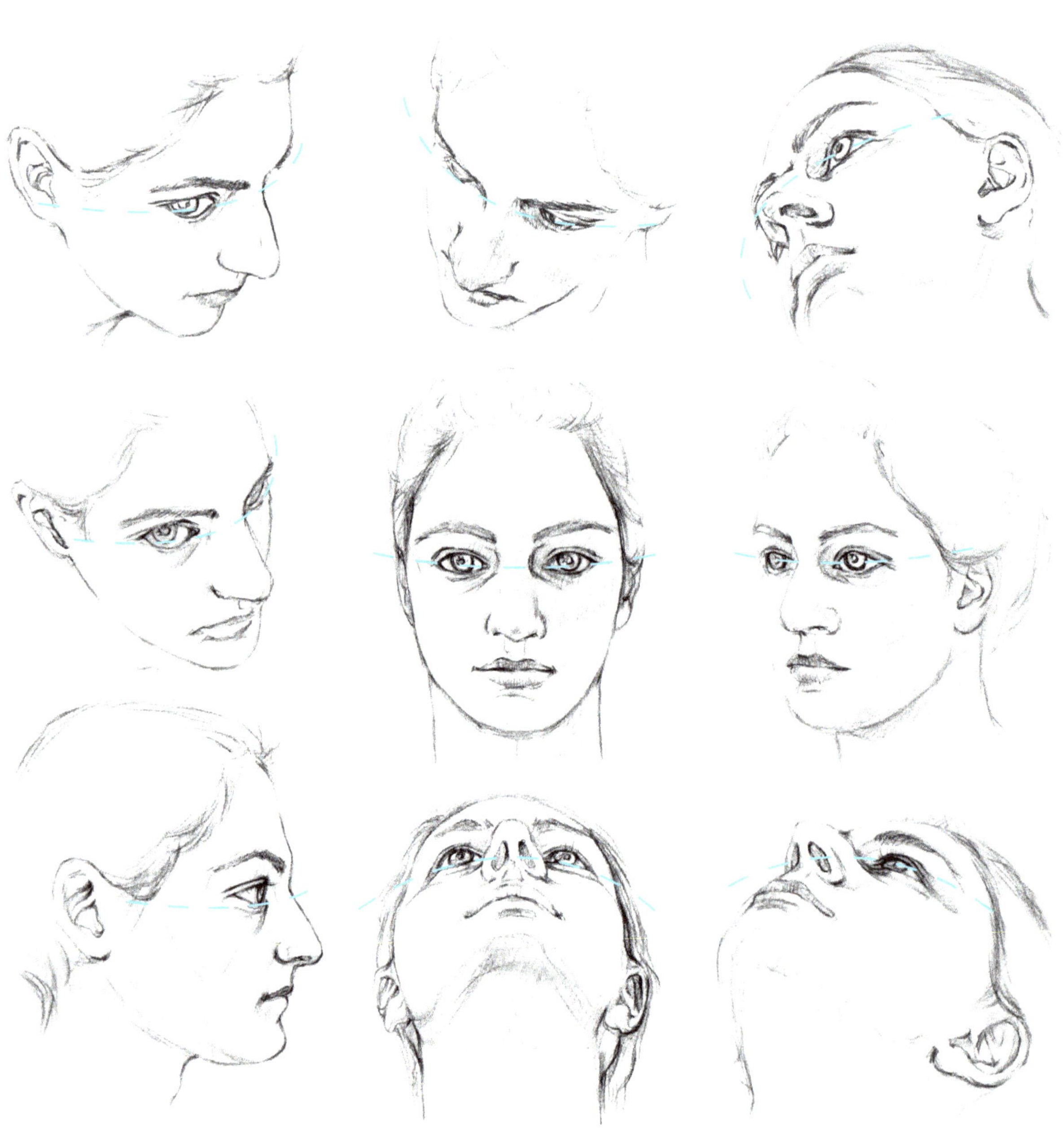

Now try drawing these basic head perspectives yourself.

The mouth consists of two main parts, the upper lip and lower lip. The lower lip is soft and rounded, receiving highlight on top and fading to shadow. The upper lip slants inward and is usually in shadow. The mouth is one of the most prominent facial features, helping us speak and express emotion. It is also very unique in shape and fullness from person to person, so it's important to pay attention to your subject's unique details.

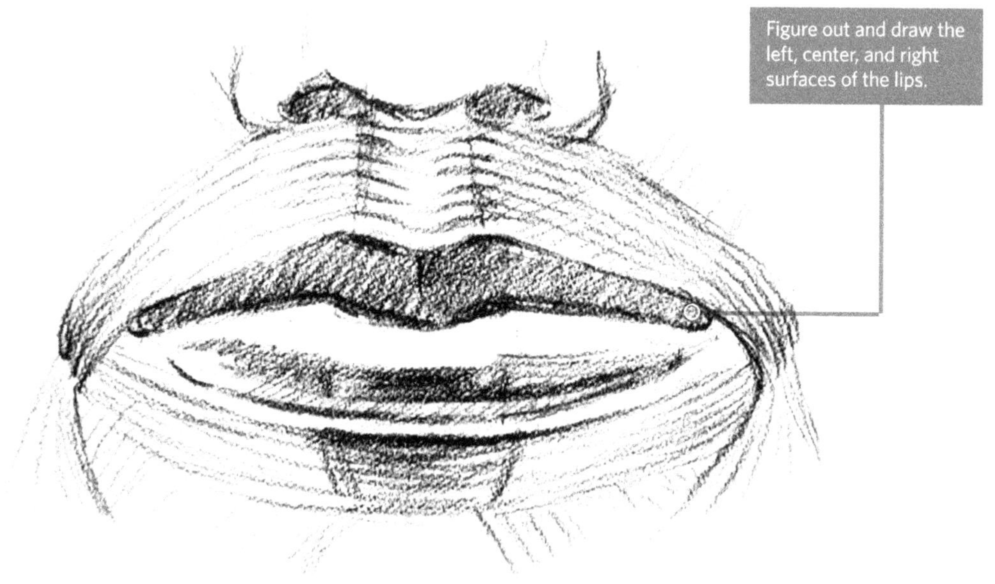

Now try drawing the basic mouth structure yourself.

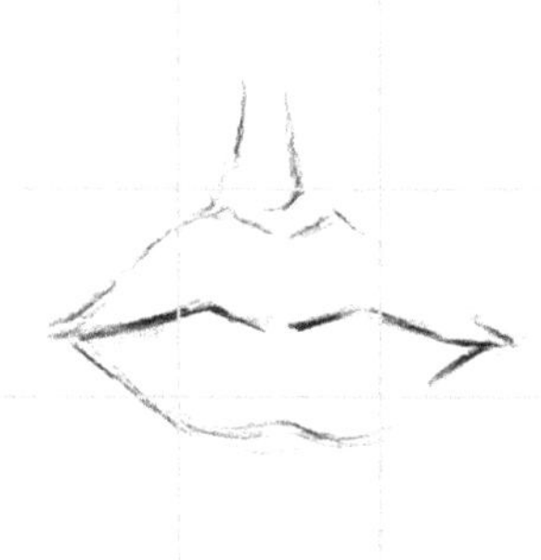

First sketch the general features of the lips in vine charcoal.

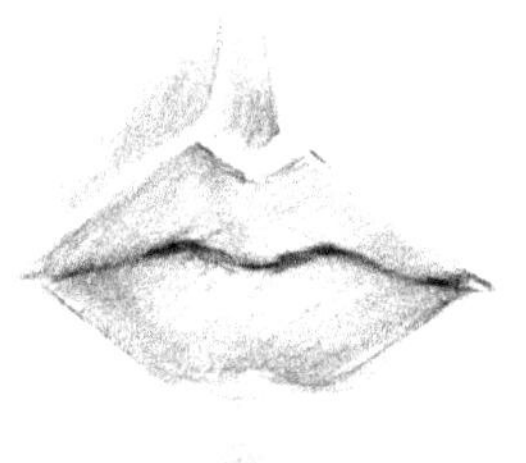

Shade in the general areas of shadow with vine charcoal.

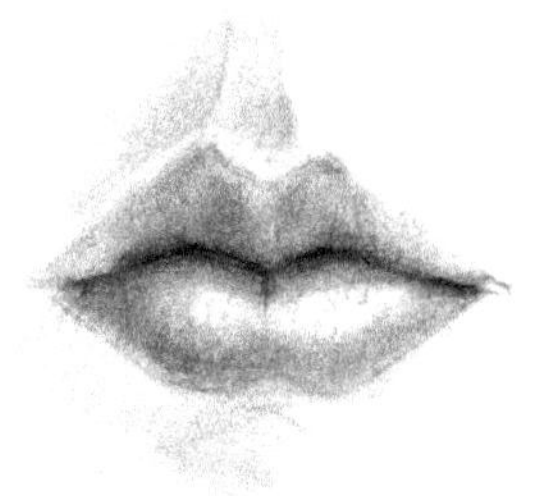

Continue to layer on vine charcoal to render more volume in the lips. Smudge areas to create a smoother skin-like texture.

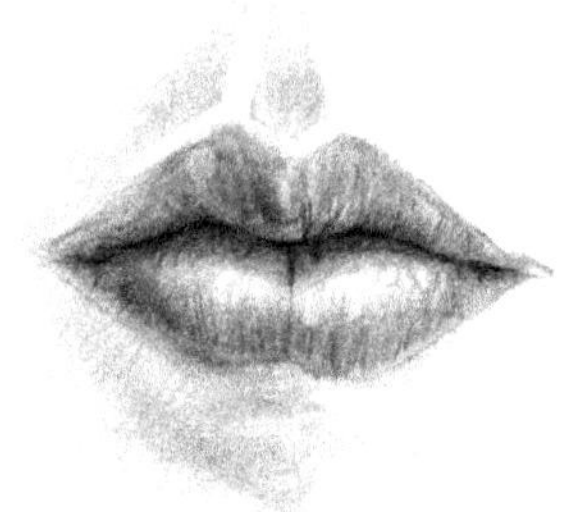

Use a bit of compressed charcoal for the darkest areas inbetween the lips. Continue to render the details of the lips and save the highlights for last by using the edge of an eraser.

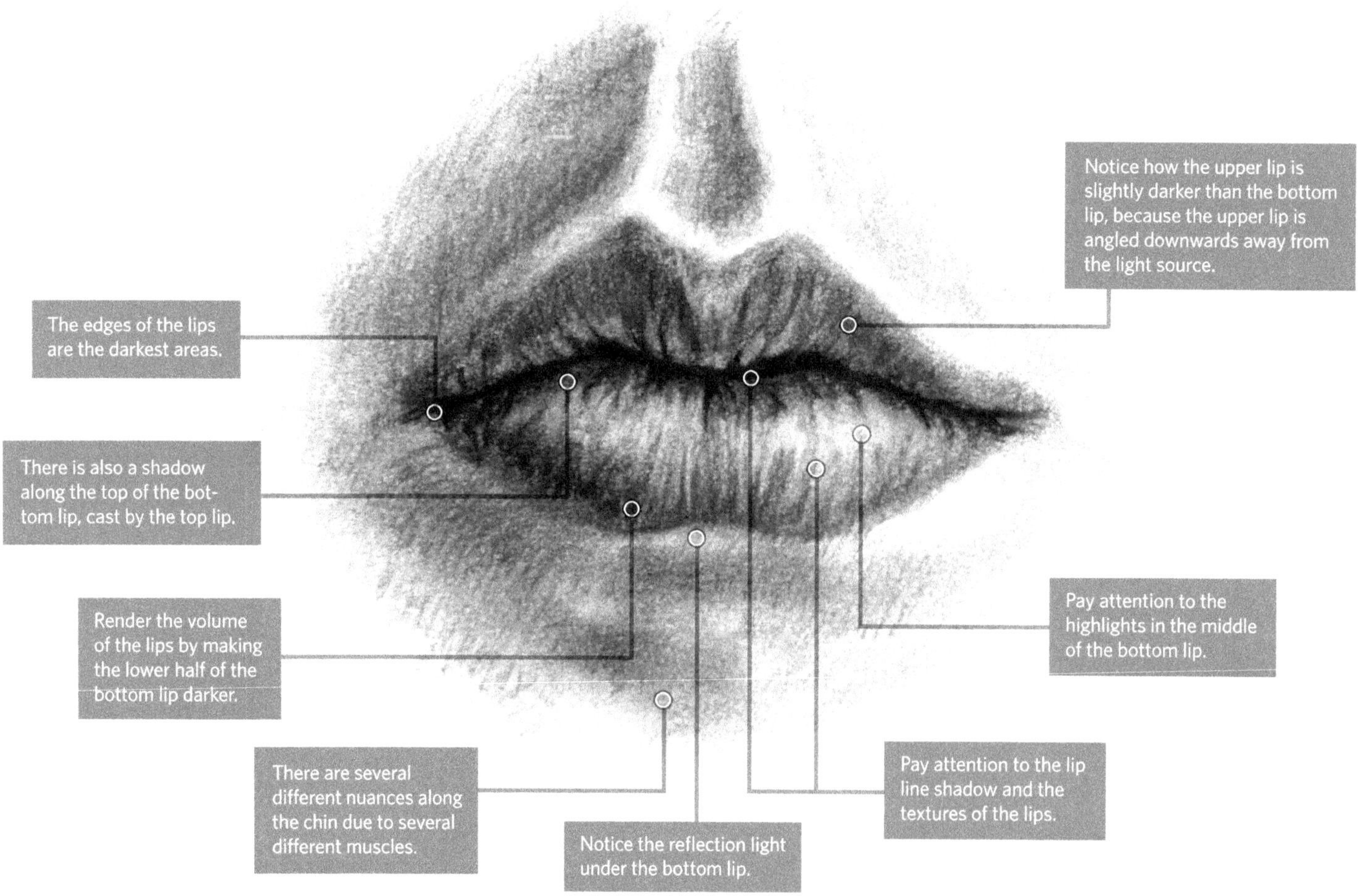

Now try drawing the front side of the mouth yourself.

Now that you have practiced how to draw the front of the mouth in charcoal following a step-by-step tutorial, use the page on the right to try and draw from life. You can draw from the picture below, use a mirror, or ask a friend to sit for you and try different variations of compositions.

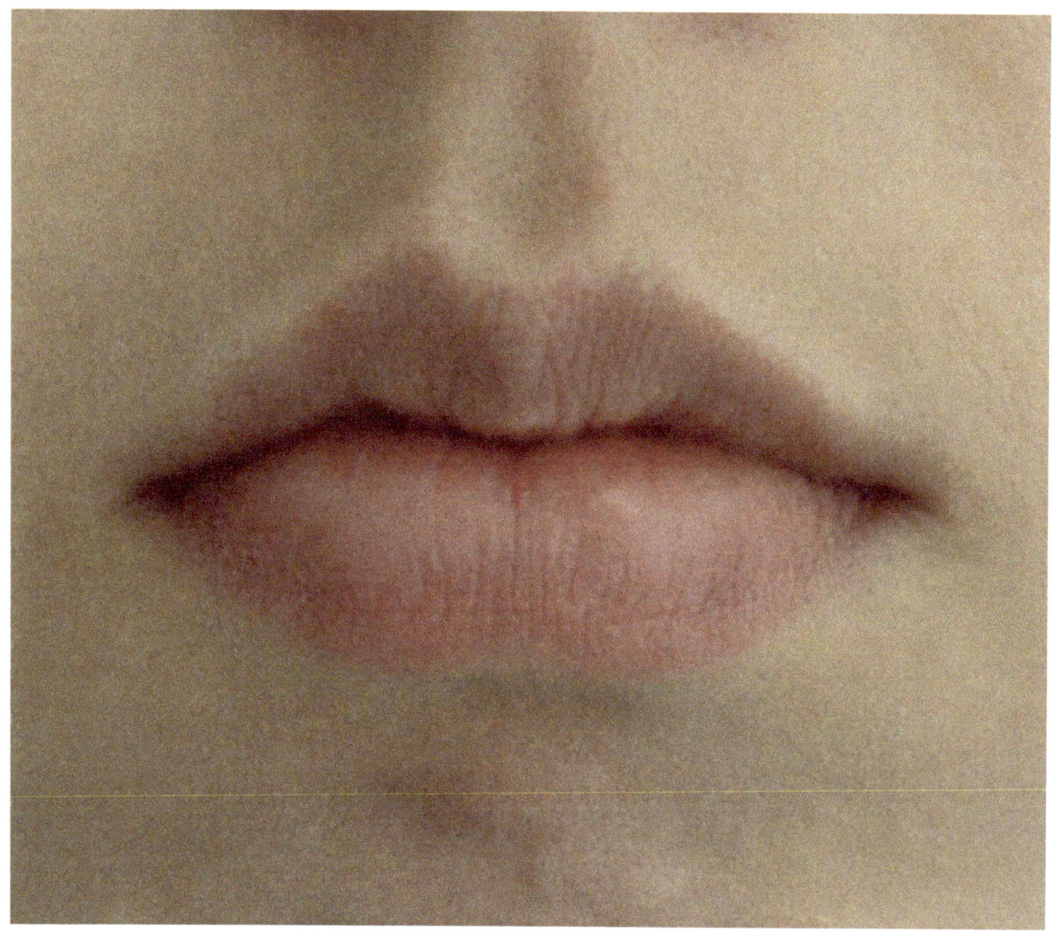

Now try drawing the front side of the mouth yourself without the grid.

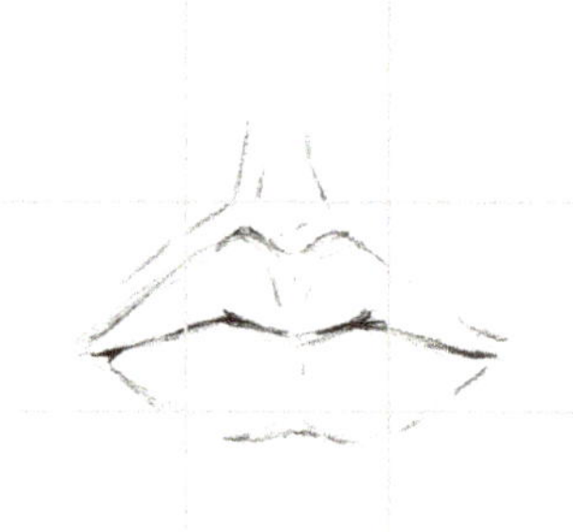

Draw the general lines to describe the shape of the lips with vine charcoal.

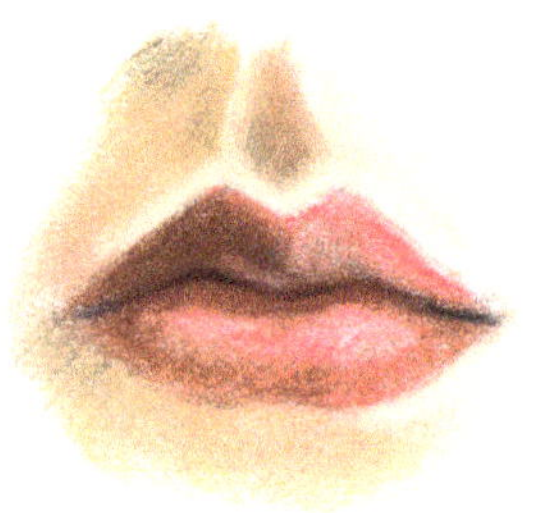

Shade in general areas of color using warm skin tones and red for the lips.

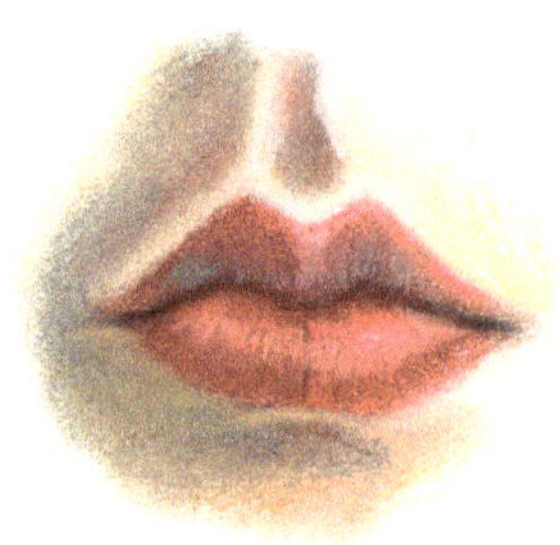

Add in more greens and blues for areas of shadow and reflection lights.

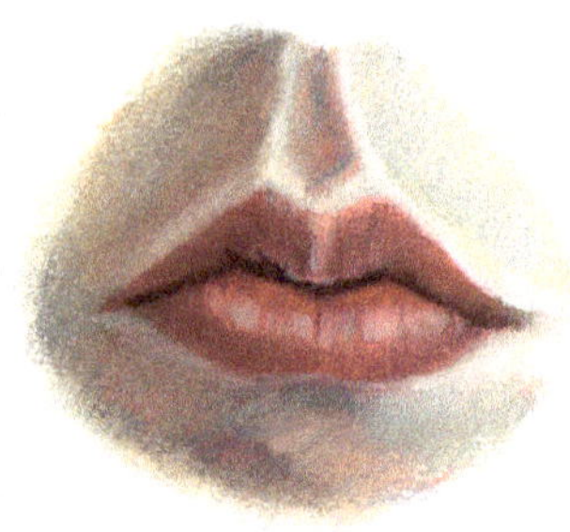

Continue to render different skin tones and lip colors to create volume and texture.

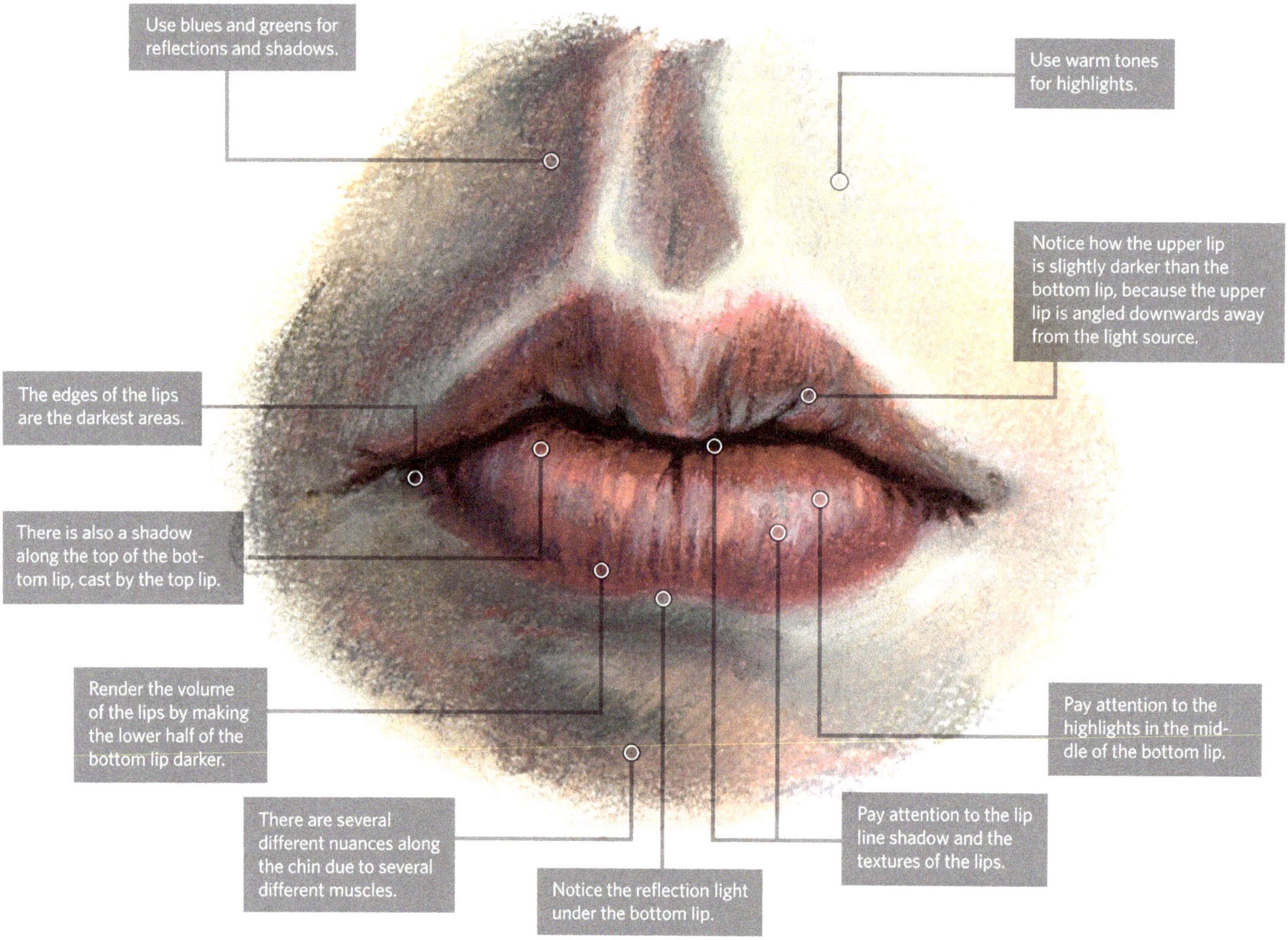

Use blues and greens for reflections and shadows.

Use warm tones for highlights.

Notice how the upper lip is slightly darker than the bottom lip, because the upper lip is angled downwards away from the light source.

The edges of the lips are the darkest areas.

There is also a shadow along the top of the bottom lip, cast by the top lip.

Render the volume of the lips by making the lower half of the bottom lip darker.

Pay attention to the highlights in the middle of the bottom lip.

There are several different nuances along the chin due to several different muscles.

Pay attention to the lip line shadow and the textures of the lips.

Notice the reflection light under the bottom lip.

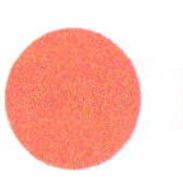
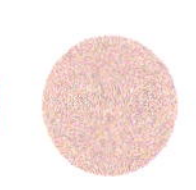

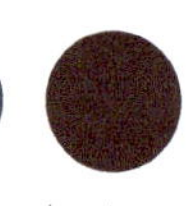
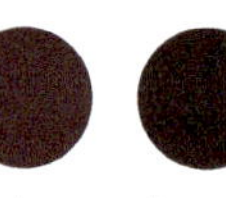

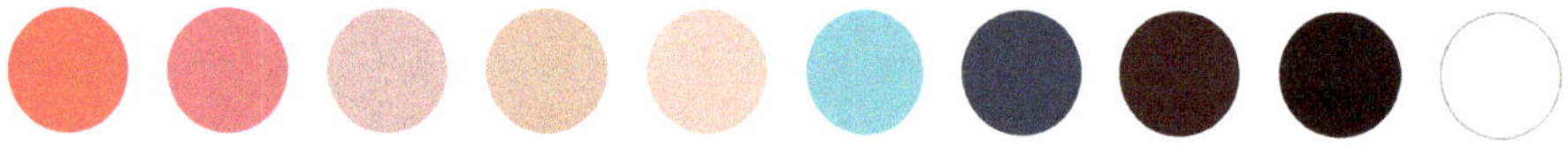

permanent red deep | carmine | permanent red | light red oxide | permanent red light | bluish green | prussian blue | burnt umber | charcoal | white

Now try drawing the front side of the mouth yourself.

Now that you have practiced how to draw the front of the mouth in pastel following a step-by-step tutorial, use the page on the right to try and draw from life. You can draw from the picture below, use a mirror, or ask a friend to sit for you and try different variations of compositions.

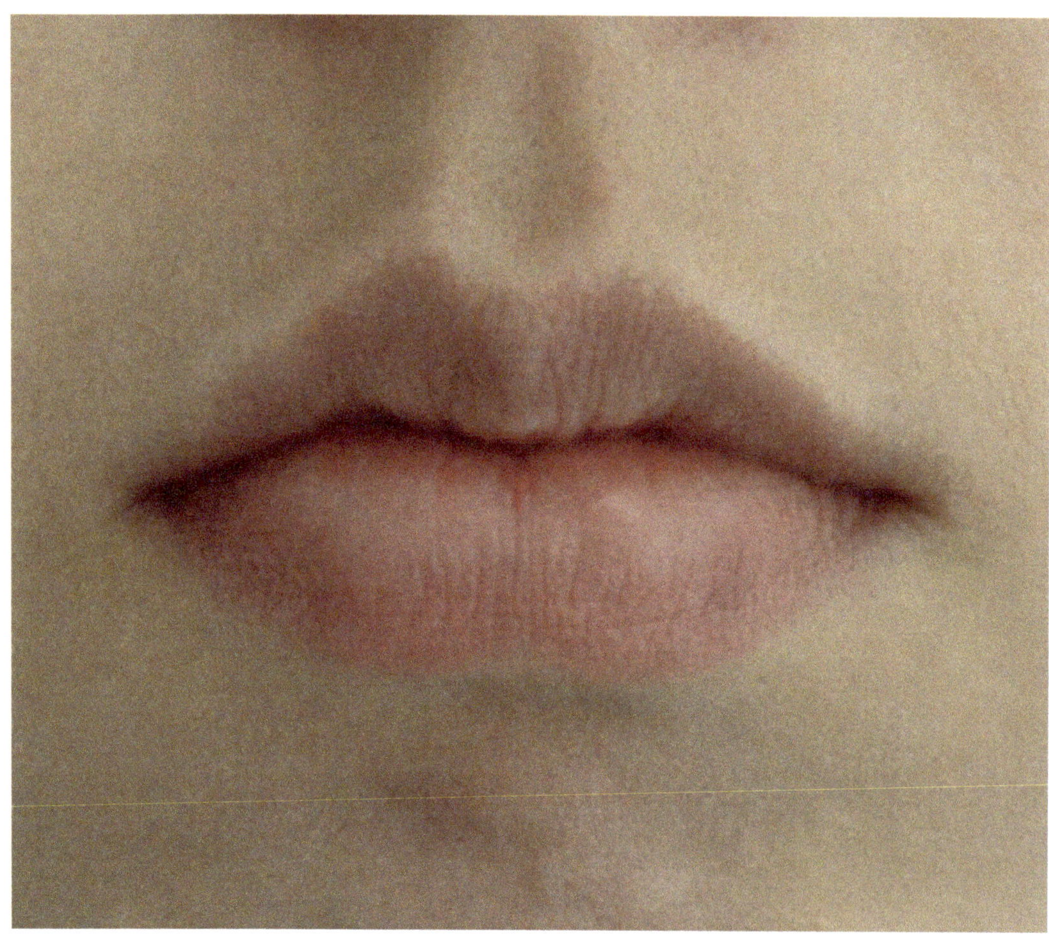

Now try drawing the front side of the mouth yourself without the grid.

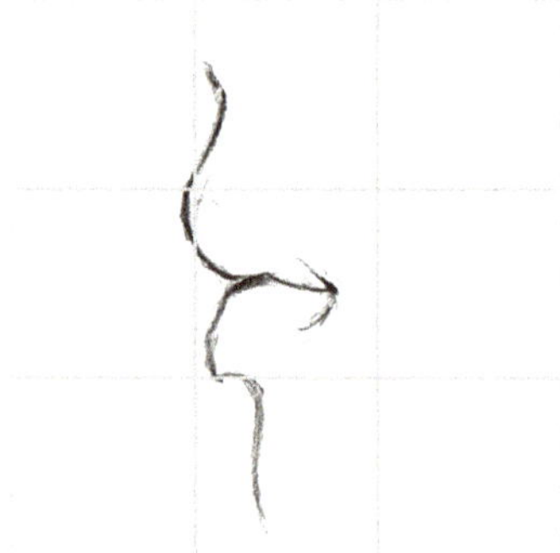

Draw the general lines to describe the shape of the lips and mouth area with vine charcoal.

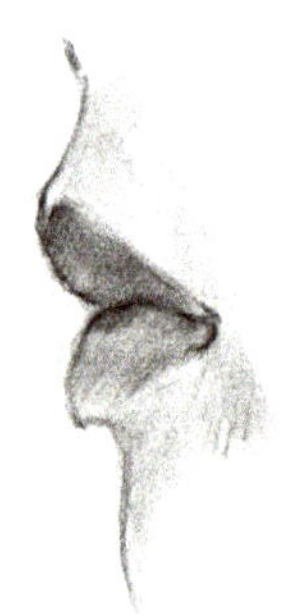

Shade in the general areas of shadow. Notice how the upper lip is slightly darker than the bottom lip.

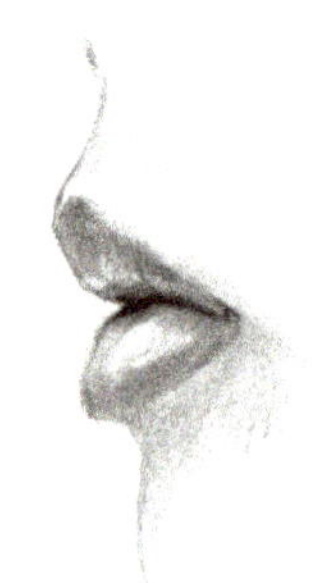

Using an eraser, create some highlights on the lips and smudge the charcoal to create the smooth texture of skin.

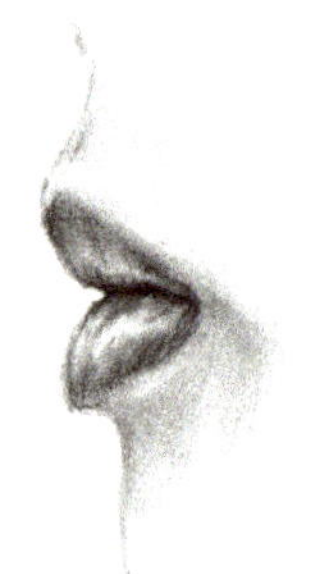

Continue to render skin tones as well as textures of the lip using a little bit of compressed charcoal and mostly vine charcoal.

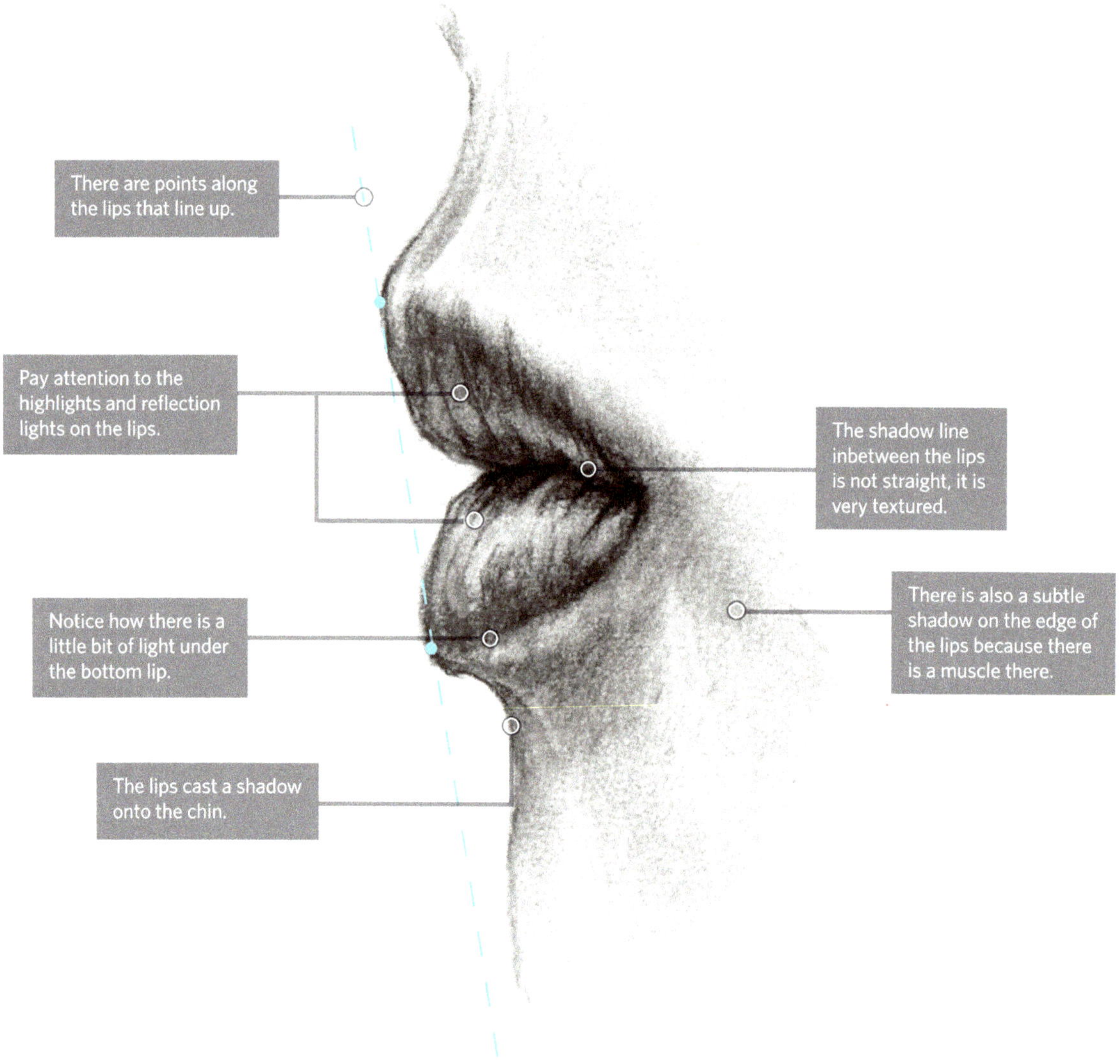

There are points along the lips that line up.

Pay attention to the highlights and reflection lights on the lips.

The shadow line inbetween the lips is not straight, it is very textured.

There is also a subtle shadow on the edge of the lips because there is a muscle there.

Notice how there is a little bit of light under the bottom lip.

The lips cast a shadow onto the chin.

Now try drawing the left side of the mouth yourself.

Now that you have practiced how to draw the left side of the mouth in charcoal following a step-by-step tutorial, use the page on the right to try and draw from life. You can draw from the picture below, use a mirror, or ask a friend to sit for you and try different variations of compositions.

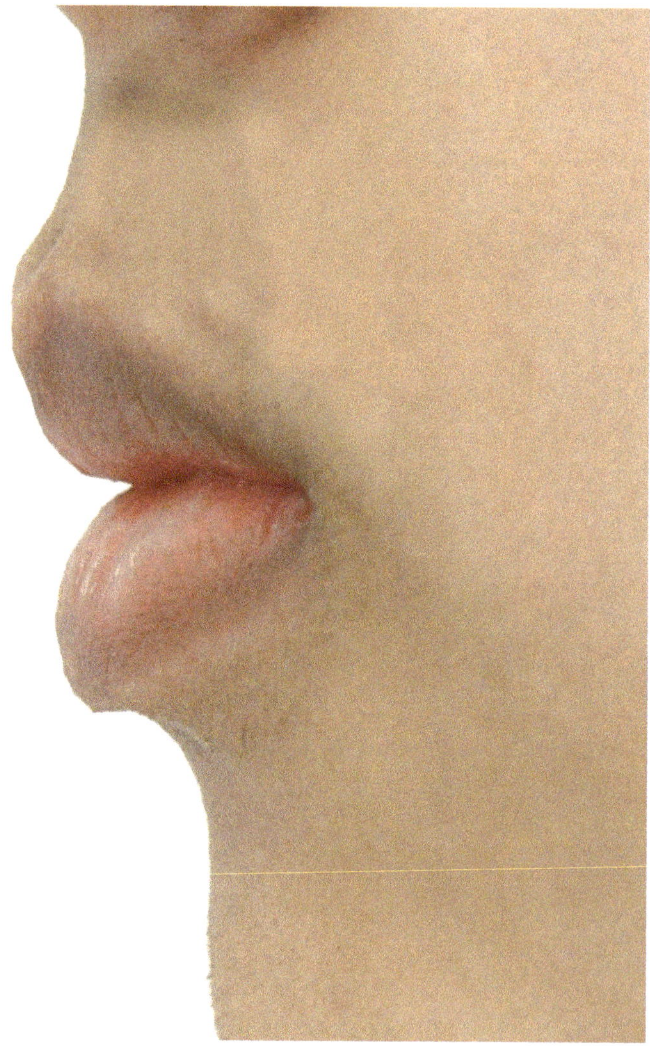

Now try drawing the left side of the mouth yourself without the grid.

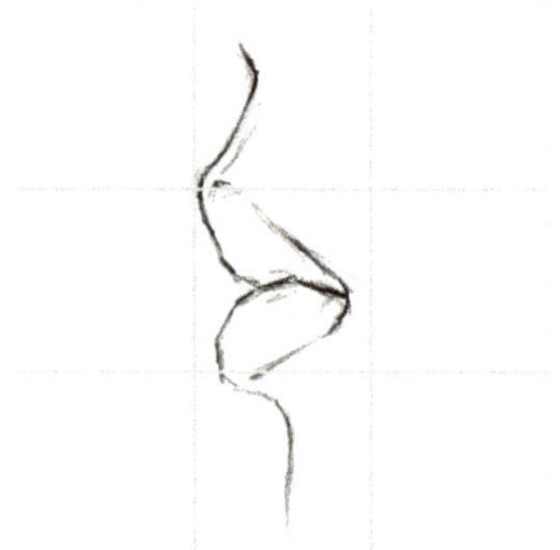

Draw the general lines to describe the shape of the lips and mouth area with vine charcoal.

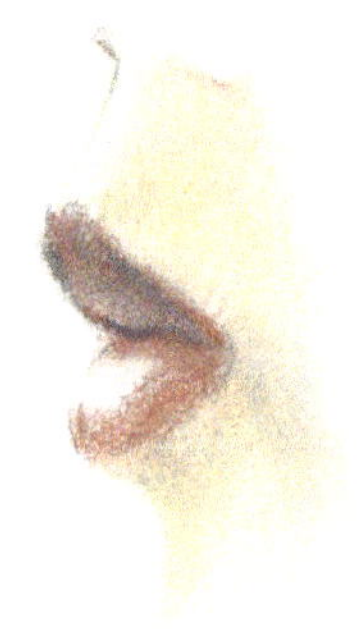

Shade in the general areas of shadow. Notice how the upper lip is slightly darker than the bottom lip.

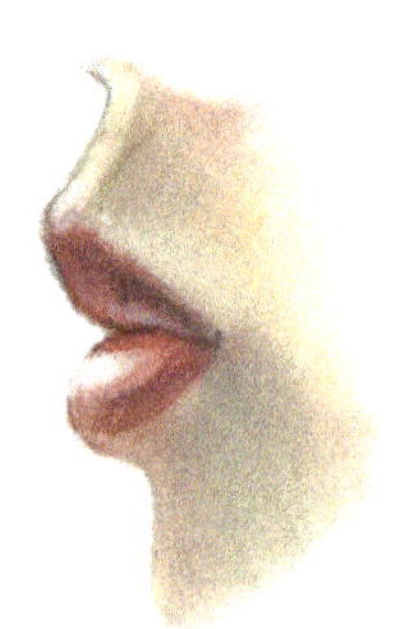

Using an eraser, create some highlights on the lips and smudge the charcoal to create the smooth texture of skin.

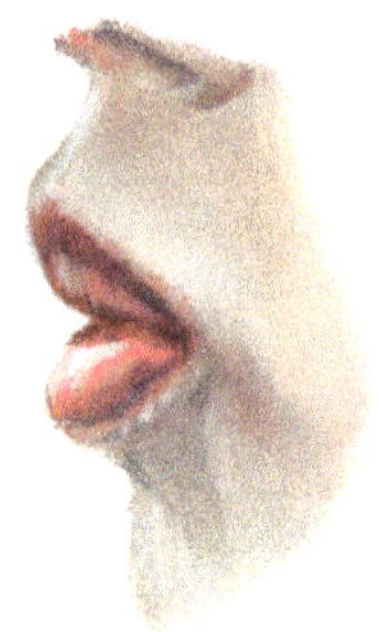

Continue to render skin tones as well as textures of the lip using a little bit of compressed charcoal and mostly vine charcoal.

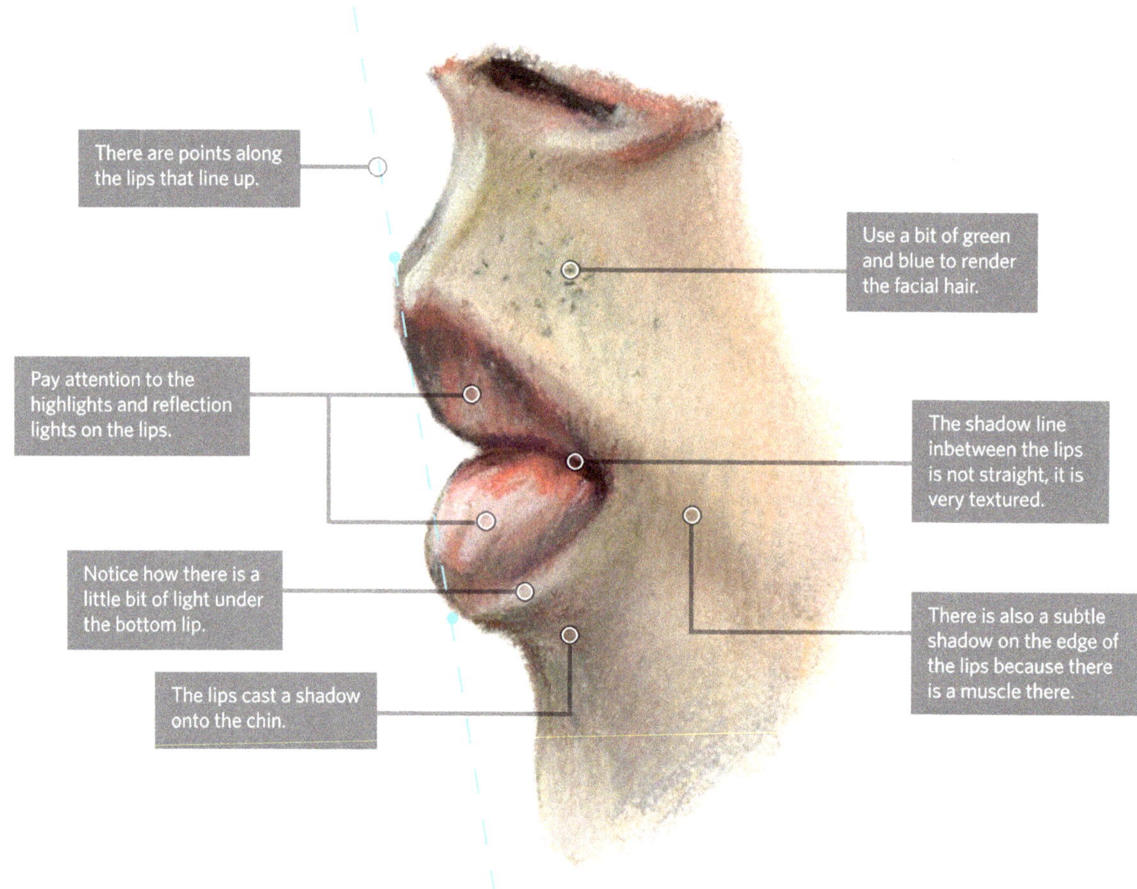

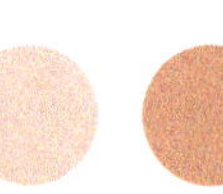
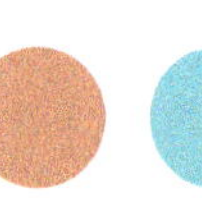

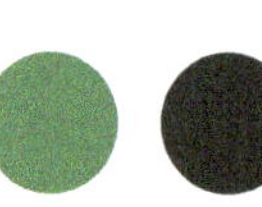
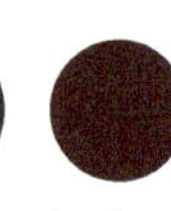

carmine | permanent red | light red oxide | permanent red light | orange | bluish green | permanent green | cinnabar green deep | burnt umber | white

Now try drawing the left side of the mouth yourself.

Now that you have practiced how to draw the left side of the mouth in pastel following a step-by-step tutorial, use the page on the right to try and draw from life. You can draw from the picture below, use a mirror, or ask a friend to sit for you and try different variations of compositions.

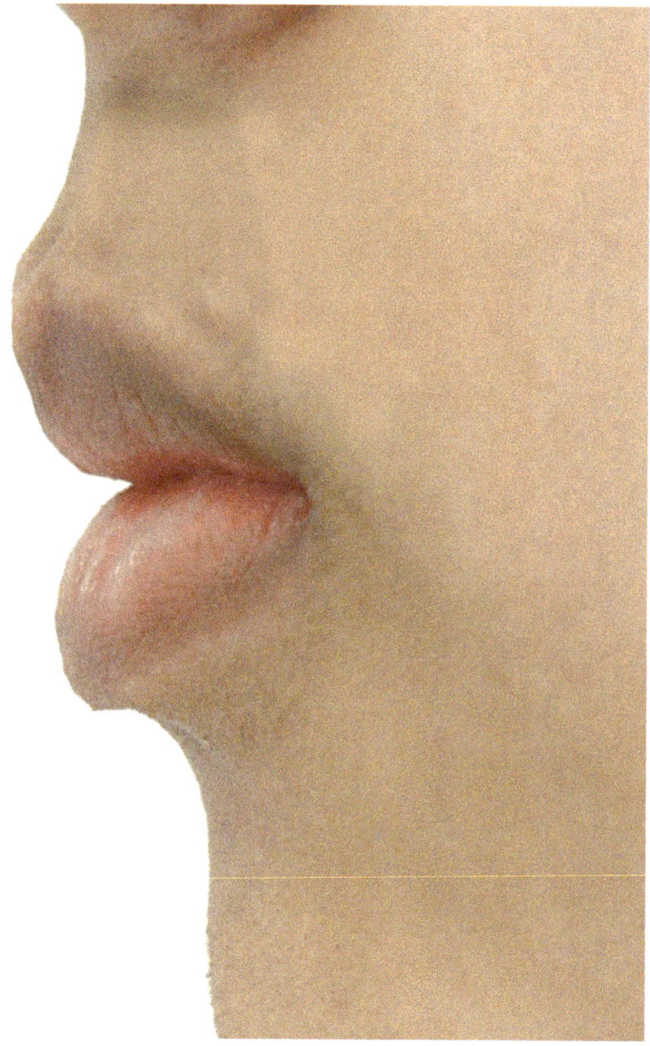

Now try drawing the left side of the mouth yourself without the grid.

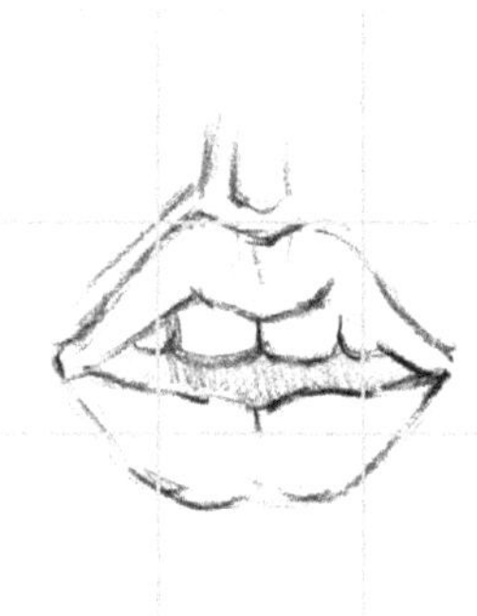

Draw the general lines to describe the shape of the lips and mouth area with vine charcoal.

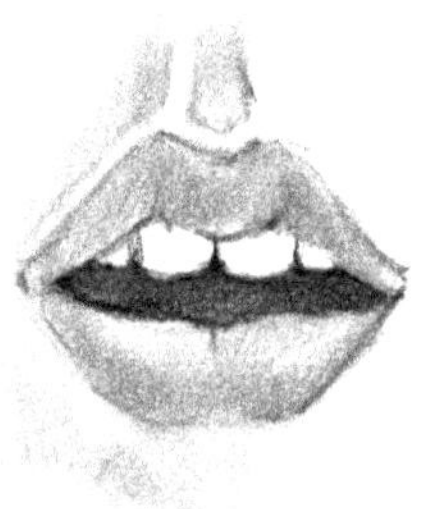

Shade in the general areas of shadow. Notice how the upper lip is slightly darker than the bottom lip.

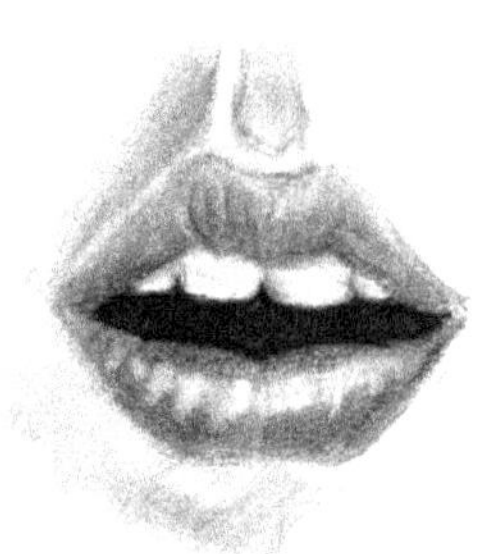

Using an eraser, create some highlights on the lips and smudge the charcoal to create the smooth texture of skin.

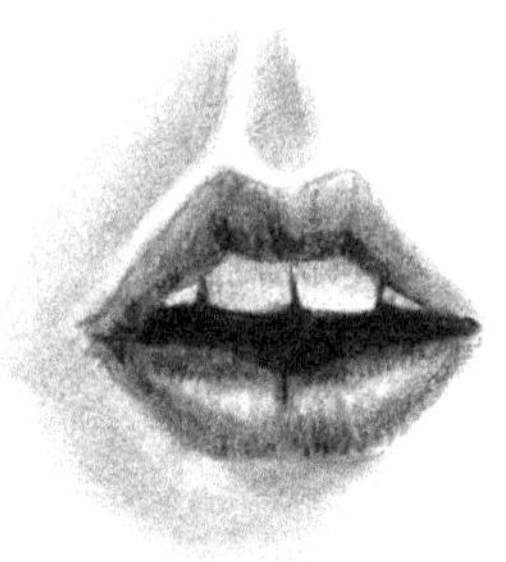

Continue to render skin tones as well as textures of the lip using a little bit of compressed charcoal and mostly vine charcoal.

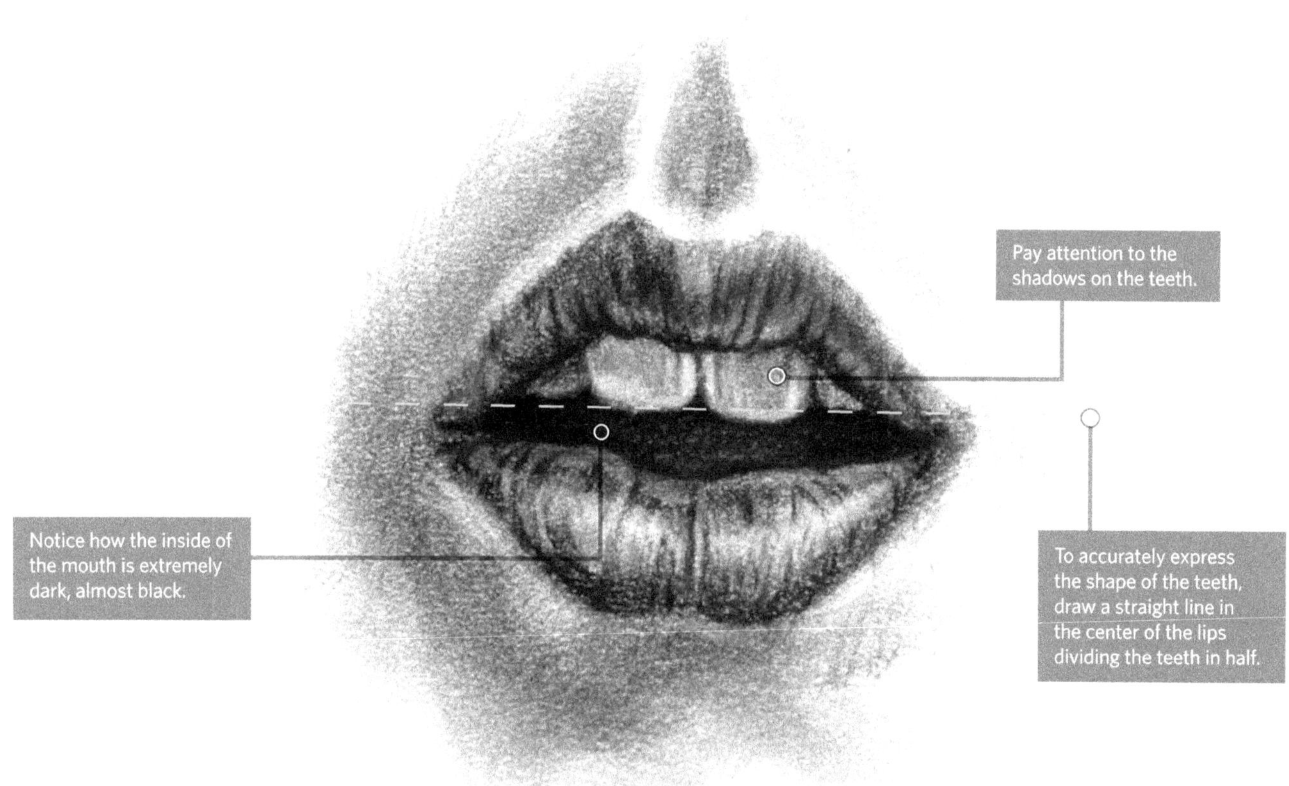

Now try drawing the slightly opened mouth yourself.

Now that you have practiced how to draw a slightly opened mouth in charcoal following a step-by-step tutorial, use the page on the right to try and draw from life. You can draw from the picture below, use a mirror, or ask a friend to sit for you and try different variations of compositions.

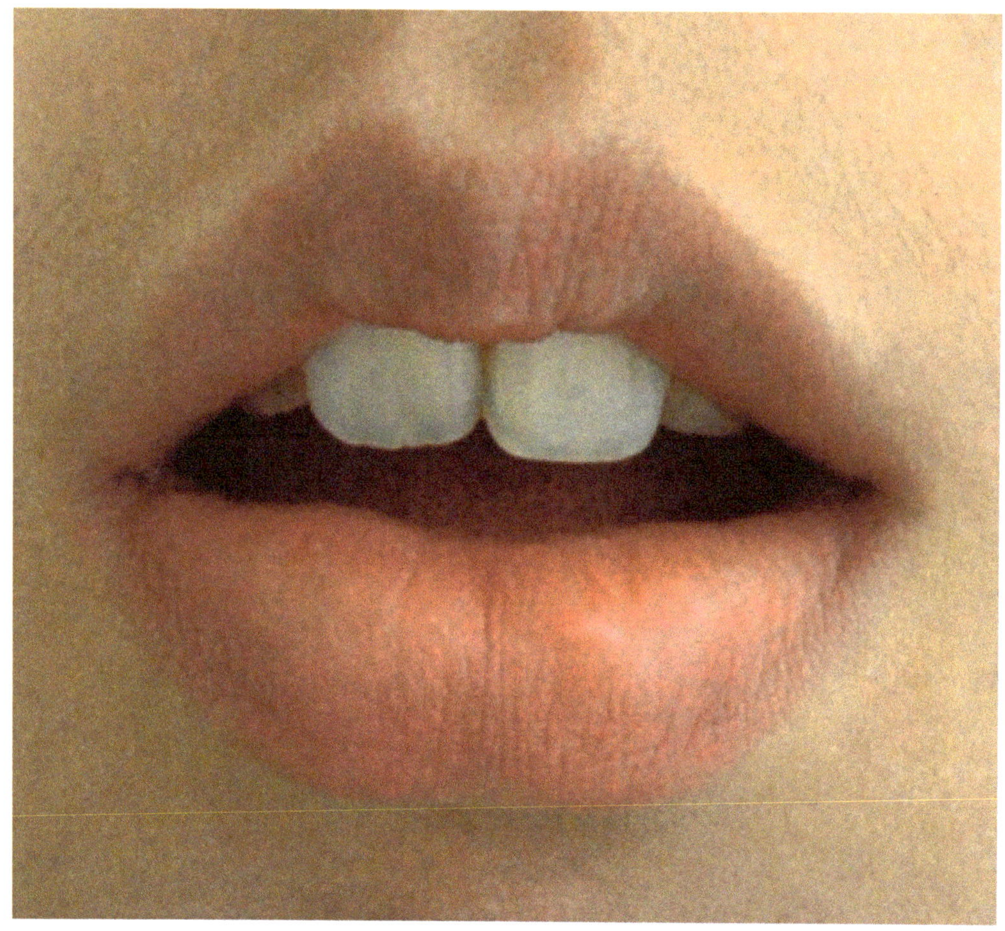

Now try drawing the slight open mouth yourself without the grid.

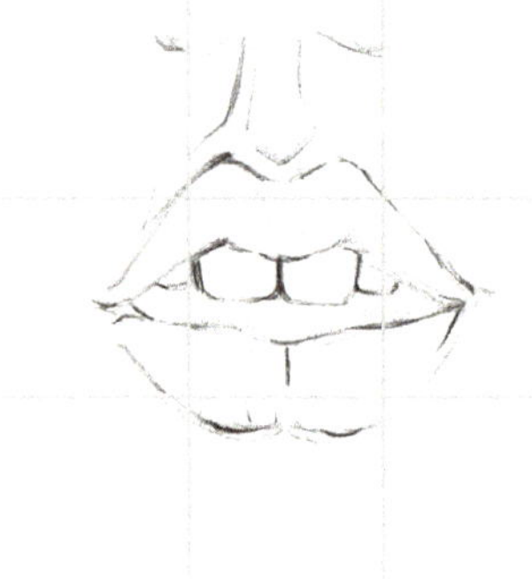

Draw the general lines to describe the shape of the lips and mouth area with vine charcoal.

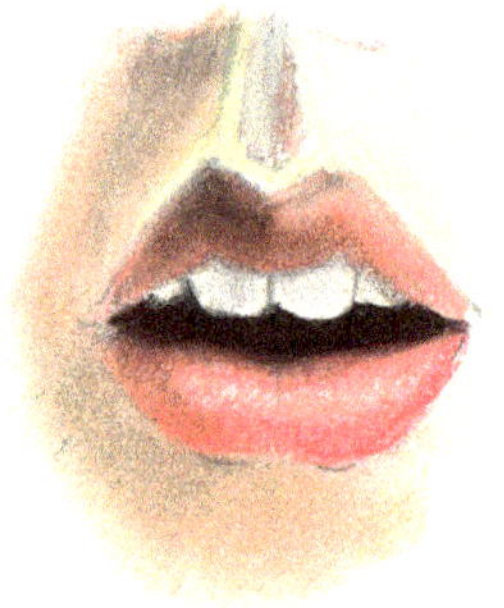

Shade in the general areas of shadow using warm skin tones and reds for the lips.. Notice how the upper lip is slightly darker than the bottom lip.

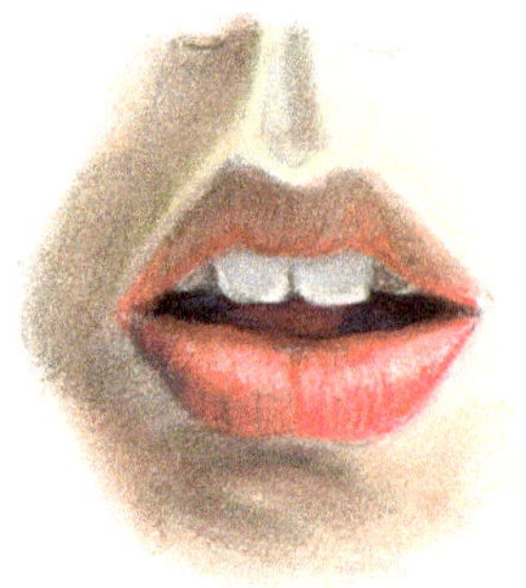

Using greens, blues and browns, render shadows. Use warm tones for highlights.

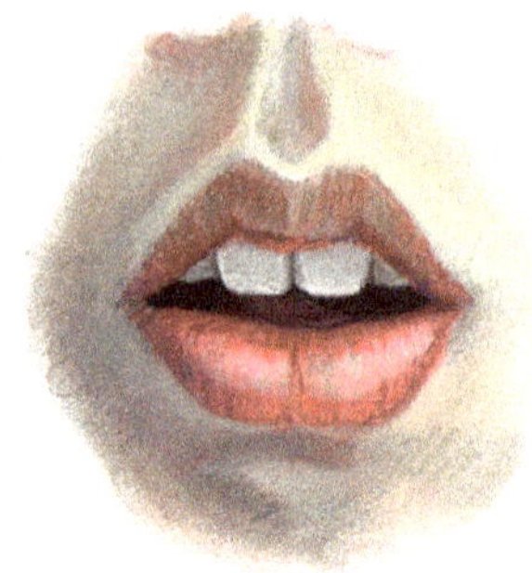

Continue to render skin tones as well as textures of the lip using more middle tones and greens, blues and browns. Smudge areas for a smoother texture.

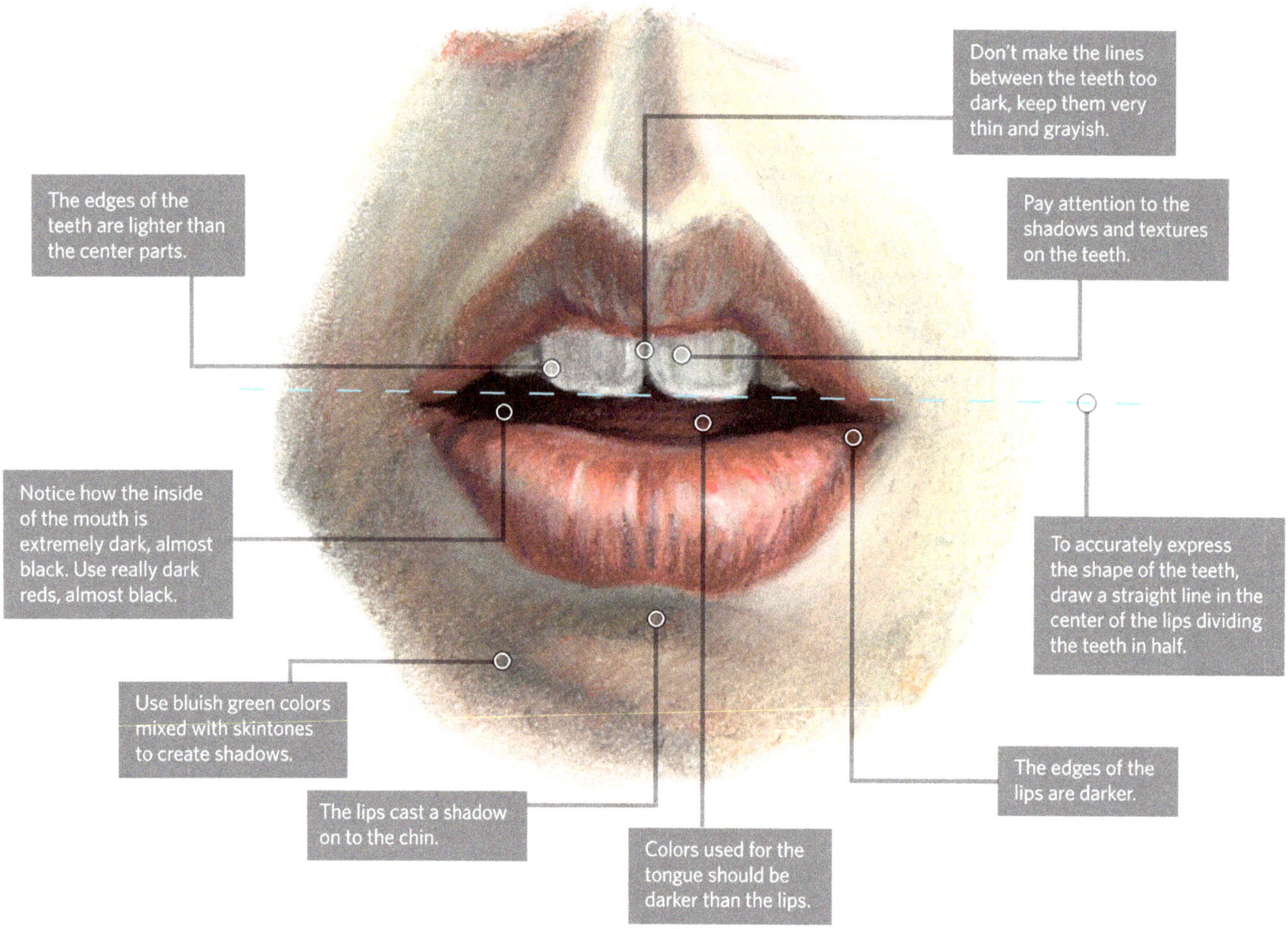

Don't make the lines between the teeth too dark, keep them very thin and grayish.

The edges of the teeth are lighter than the center parts.

Pay attention to the shadows and textures on the teeth.

Notice how the inside of the mouth is extremely dark, almost black. Use really dark reds, almost black.

To accurately express the shape of the teeth, draw a straight line in the center of the lips dividing the teeth in half.

Use bluish green colors mixed with skintones to create shadows.

The edges of the lips are darker.

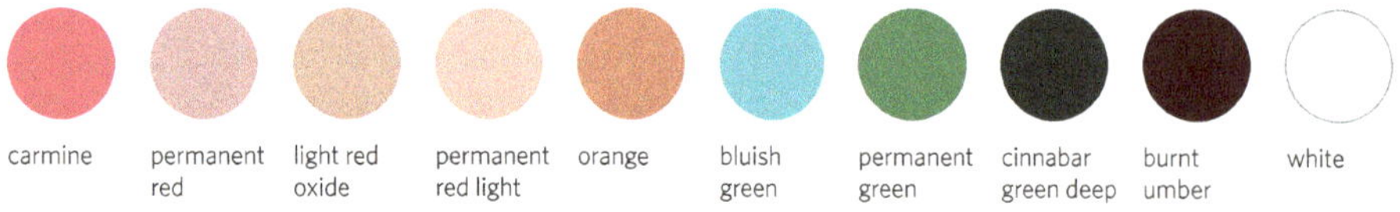

The lips cast a shadow on to the chin.

Colors used for the tongue should be darker than the lips.

carmine

permanent red

light red oxide

permanent red light

orange

bluish green

permanent green

cinnabar green deep

burnt umber

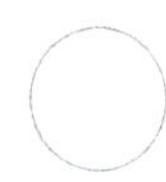

white

Now try drawing the slightly opened mouth yourself.

Now that you have practiced how to draw a slightly opened mouth in pastel following a step-by-step tutorial, use the page on the right to try and draw from life. You can draw from the picture below, use a mirror, or ask a friend to sit for you and try different variations of compositions.

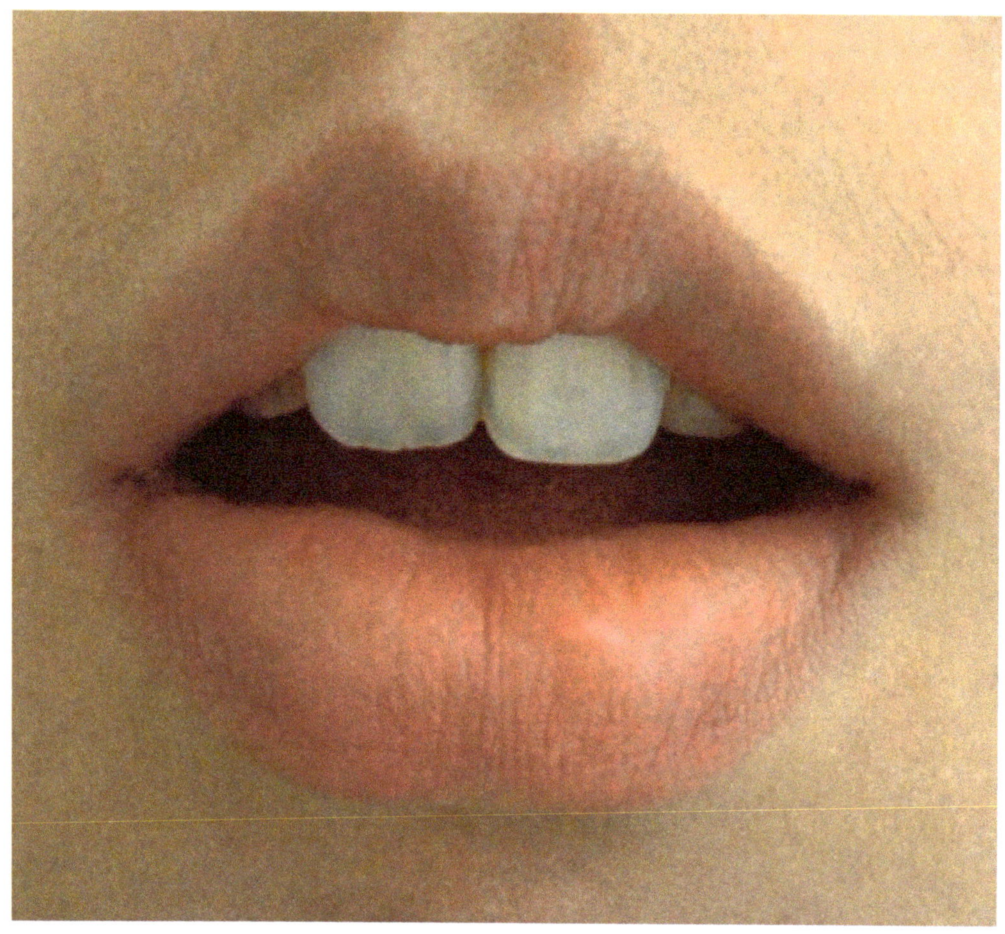

Now try drawing the slight open mouth yourself without the grid.

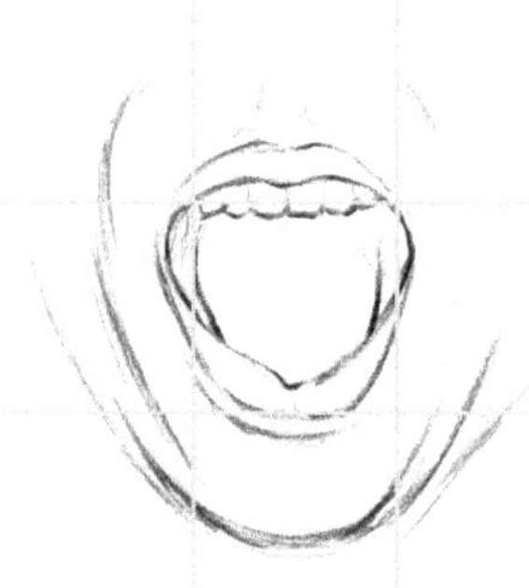

Draw the general lines to describe the shape of the lips and mouth area with vine charcoal.

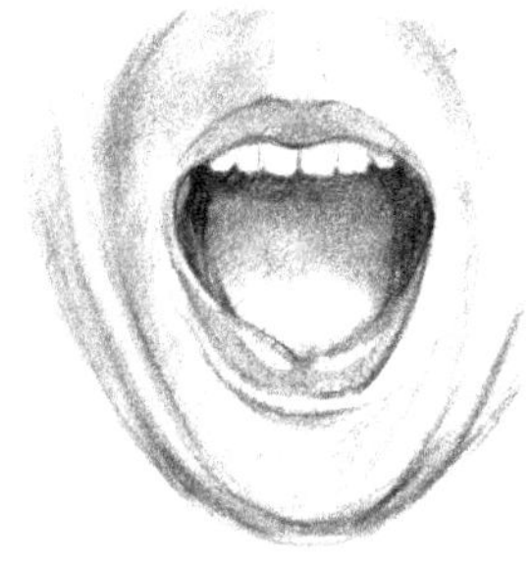

Shade in the general areas of shadow. Notice how the upper lip is slightly darker than the bottom lip.

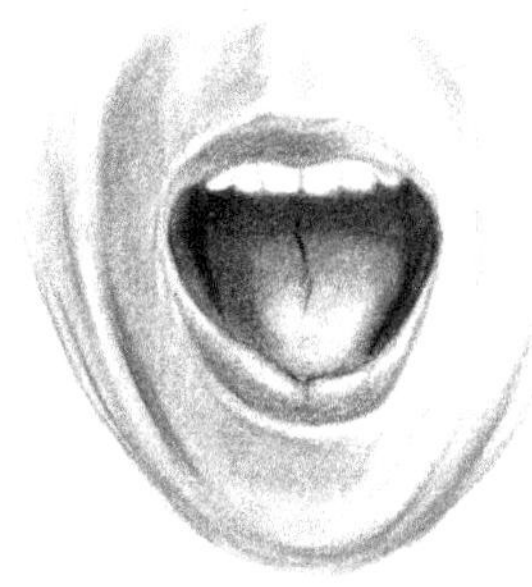

Using an eraser, create some highlights on the lips and smudge the charcoal to create the smooth texture of skin.

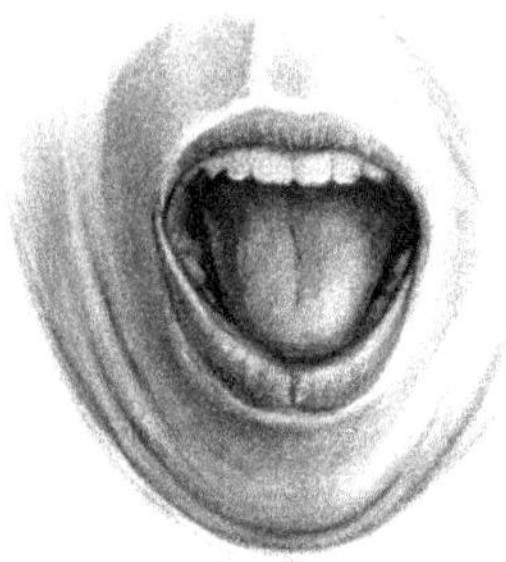

Continue to render skin tones as well as textures of the lip using a little bit of compressed charcoal and mostly vine charcoal.

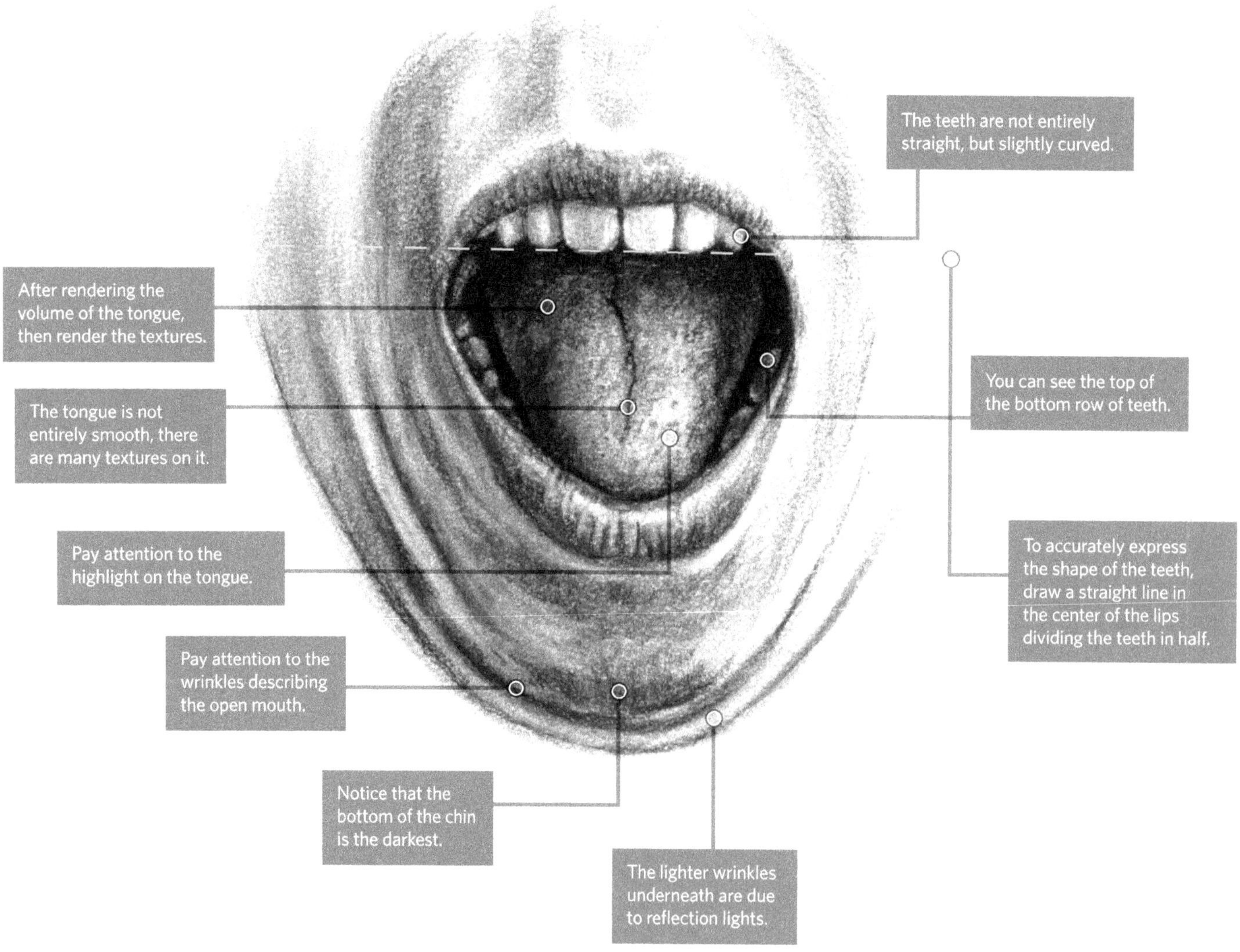

The teeth are not entirely straight, but slightly curved.

After rendering the volume of the tongue, then render the textures.

You can see the top of the bottom row of teeth.

The tongue is not entirely smooth, there are many textures on it.

Pay attention to the highlight on the tongue.

To accurately express the shape of the teeth, draw a straight line in the center of the lips dividing the teeth in half.

Pay attention to the wrinkles describing the open mouth.

Notice that the bottom of the chin is the darkest.

The lighter wrinkles underneath are due to reflection lights.

Now try drawing the wide open mouth yourself.

Now that you have practiced how to draw a wide opened mouth in charcoal following a step-by-step tutorial, use the page on the right to try and draw from life. You can draw from the picture below, use a mirror, or ask a friend to sit for you and try different variations of compositions.

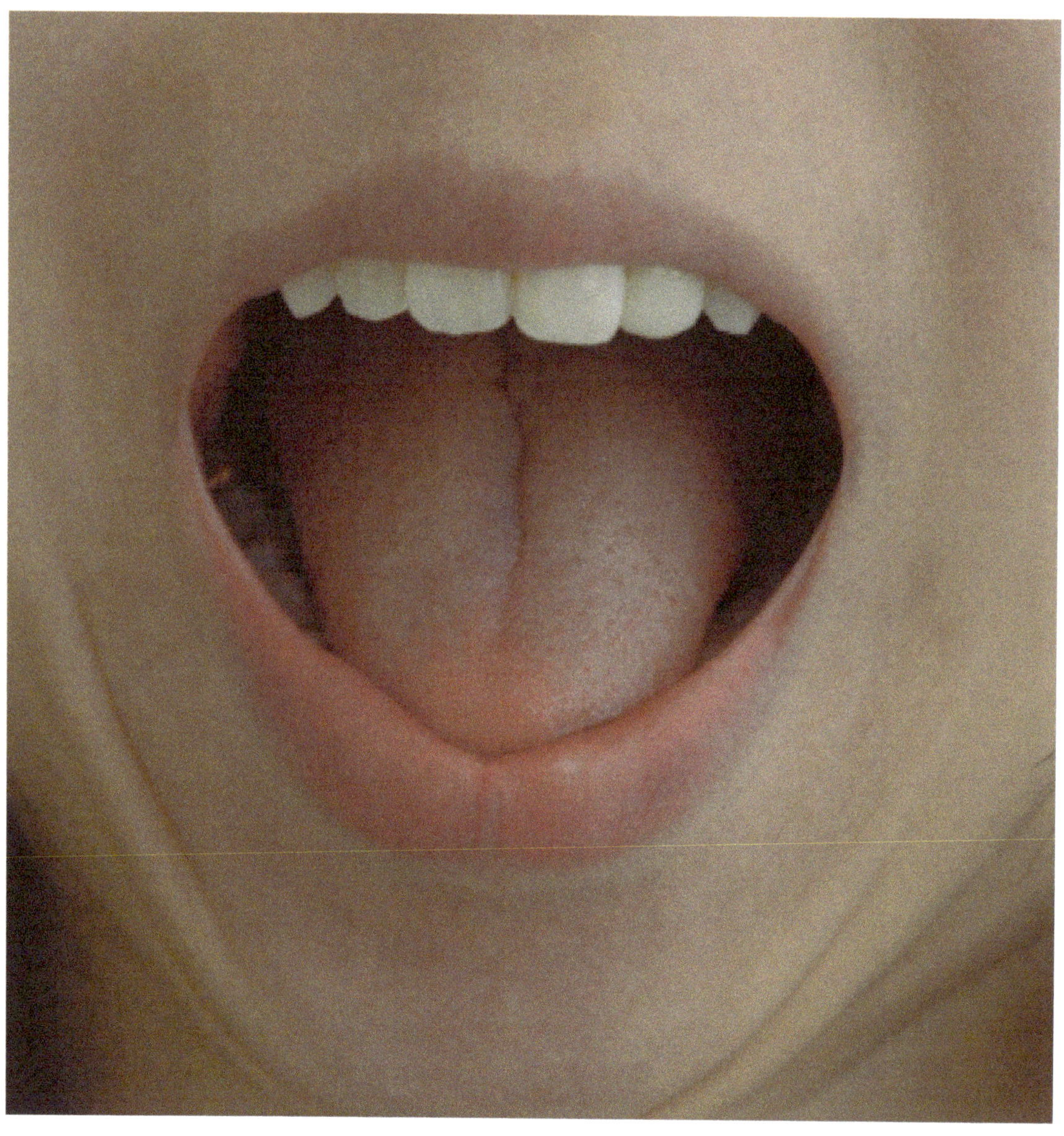

Now try drawing the wide open mouth yourself without the grid.

WIDE OPEN MOUTH IN PASTEL: TIPS

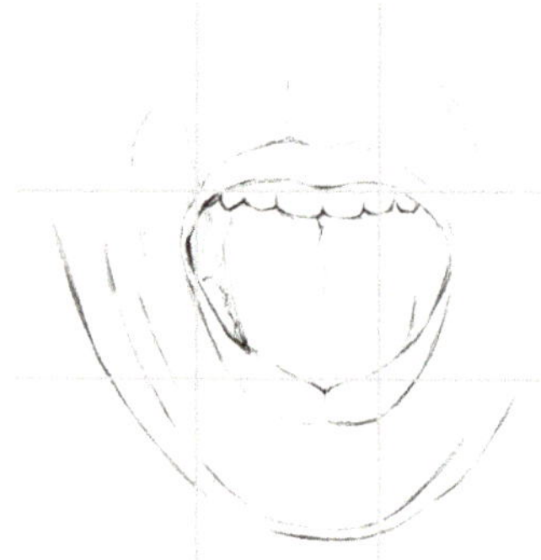

Draw the general lines to describe the shape of the lips and mouth area with vine charcoal.

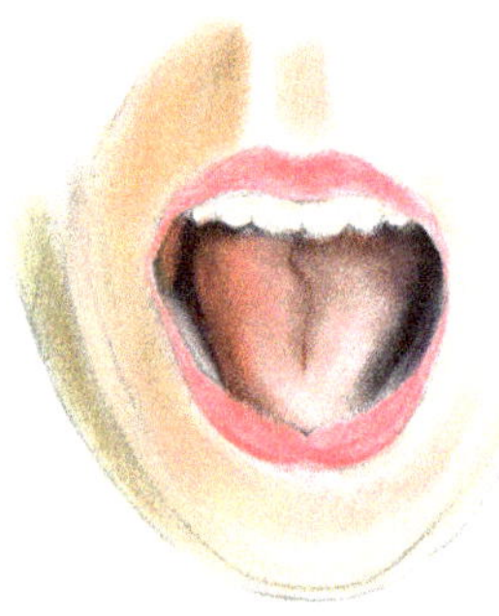

Shade in the general areas of shadow using warm skin tones and reds for the lips.. Notice how the upper lip is slightly darker than the bottom lip.

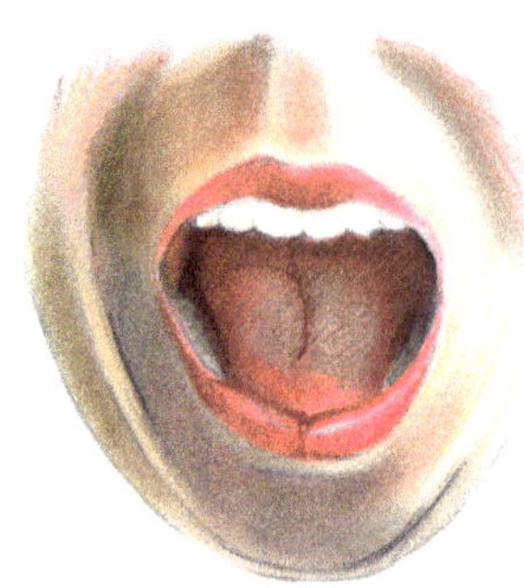

Using greens, blues and browns, render shadows. Use warm tones for highlights.

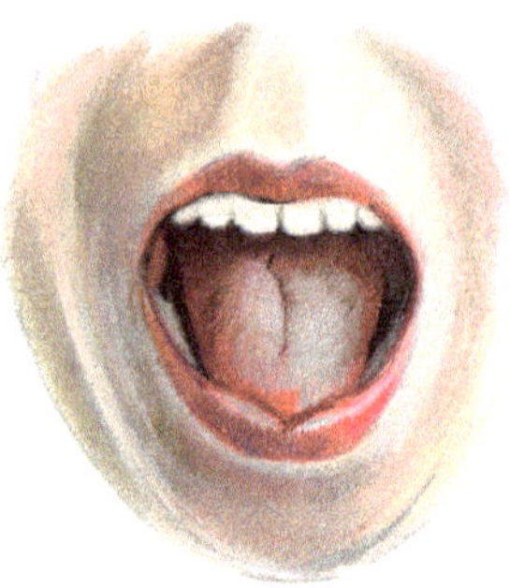

Continue to render skin tones as well as textures of the lip using more middle tones and greens, blues and browns. Smudge areas

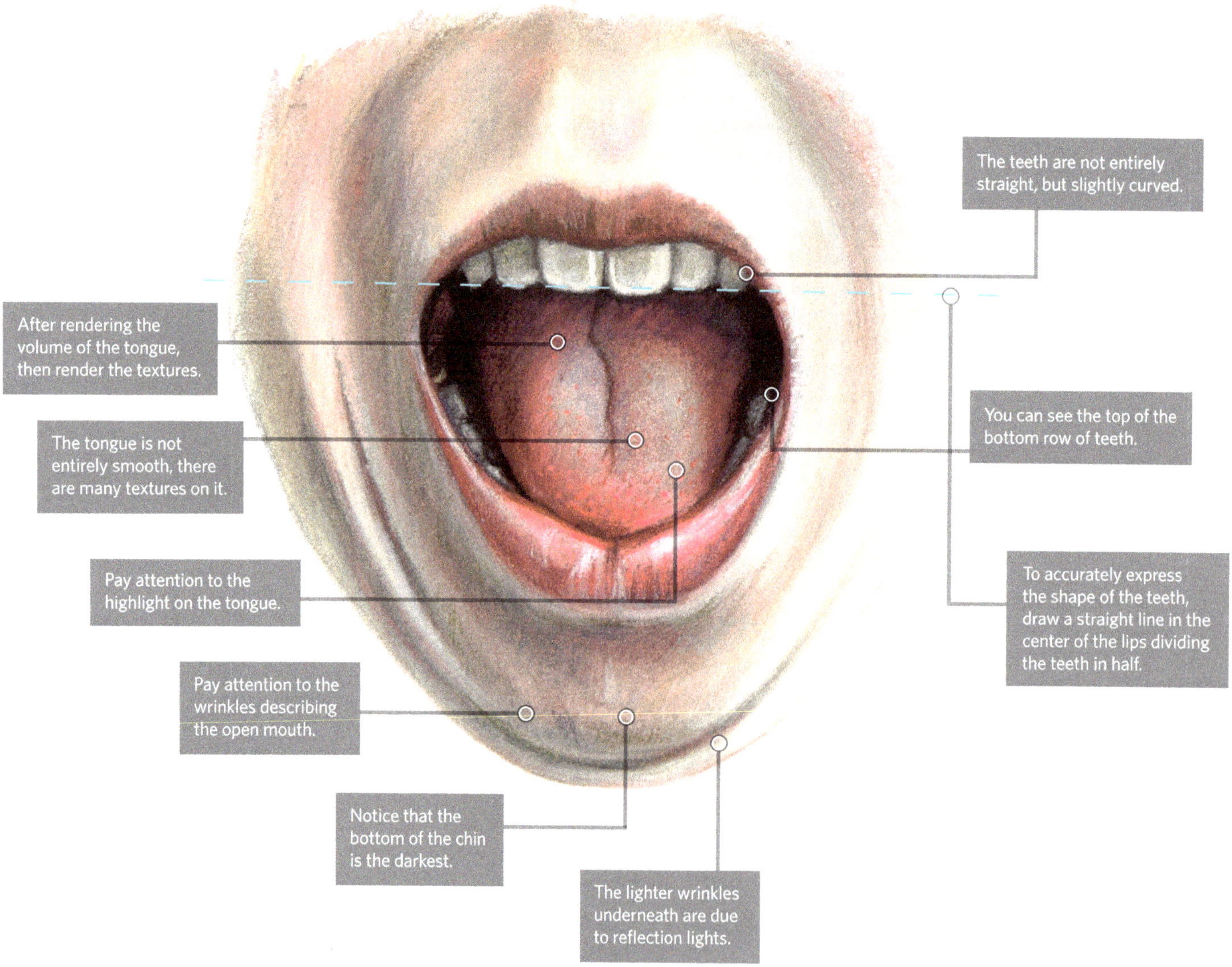

After rendering the volume of the tongue, then render the textures.

The tongue is not entirely smooth, there are many textures on it.

Pay attention to the highlight on the tongue.

Pay attention to the wrinkles describing the open mouth.

Notice that the bottom of the chin is the darkest.

The lighter wrinkles underneath are due to reflection lights.

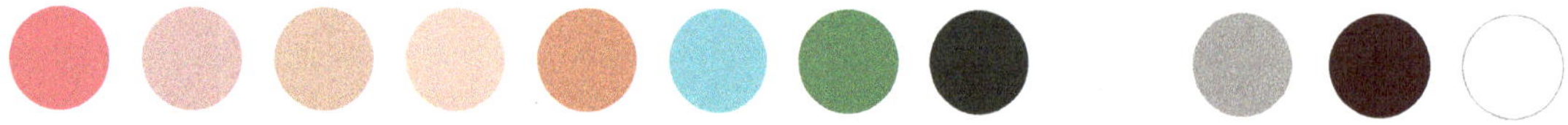

The teeth are not entirely straight, but slightly curved.

You can see the top of the bottom row of teeth.

To accurately express the shape of the teeth, draw a straight line in the center of the lips dividing the teeth in half.

carmine, permanent red, light red oxide, permanent red light, orange, bluish green, permanent green, cinnabar green deep, green gray, green gray, burnt umber, white

Now try drawing the swide open mouth yourself.

Now that you have practiced how to draw a wide opened mouth in pastel following a step-by-step tutorial, use the page on the right to try and draw from life. You can draw from the picture below, use a mirror, or ask a friend to sit for you and try different variations of compositions.

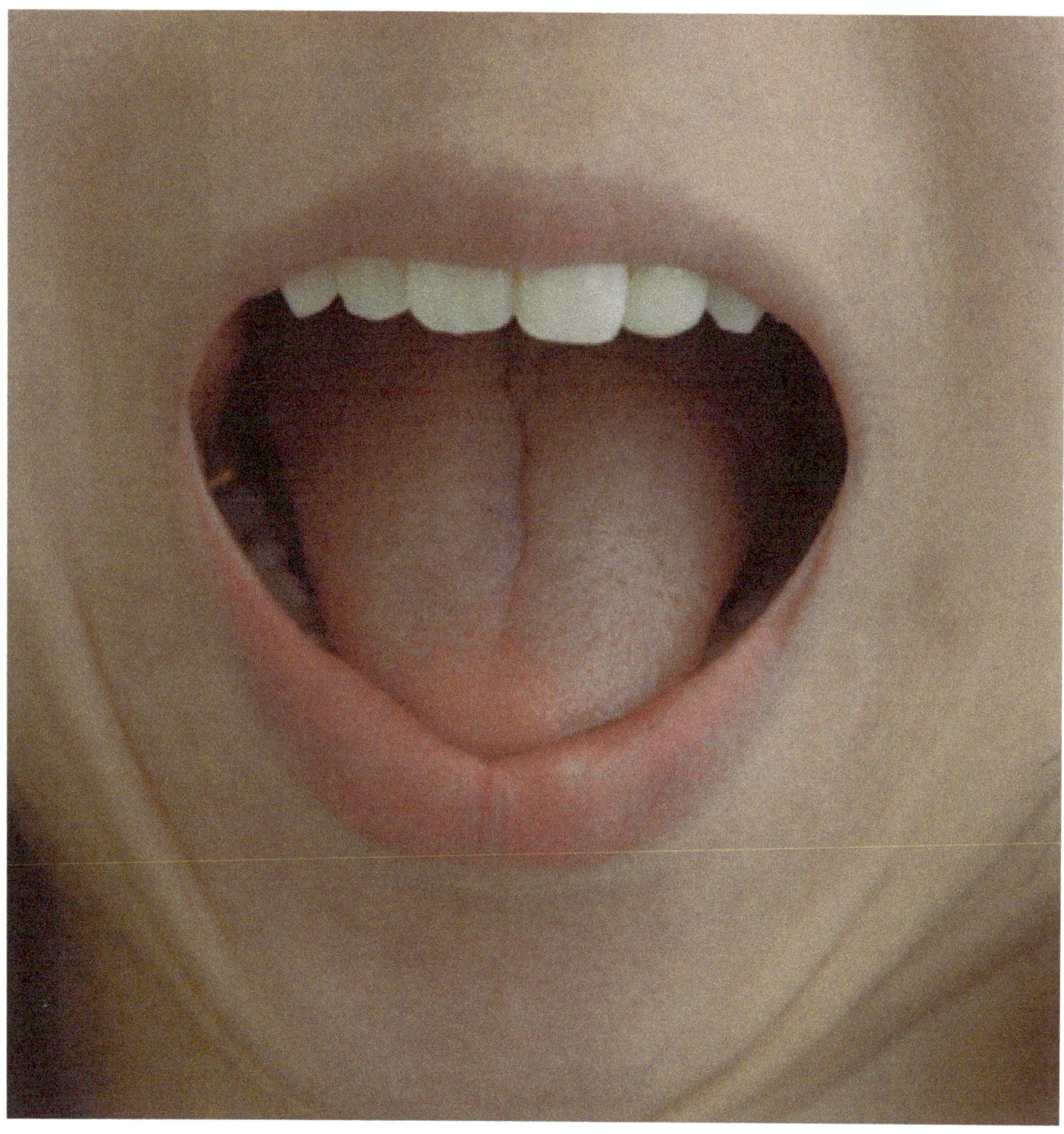

Now try drawing the wide open mouth yourself without the grid.

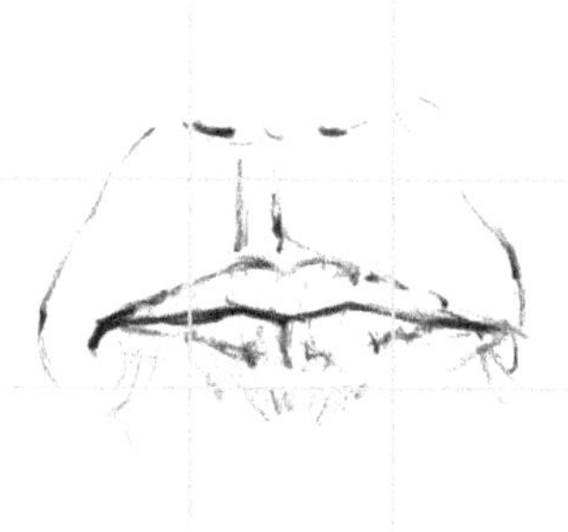

Draw the general lines to describe the shape of the lips and mouth area, as well as the frown line with vine charcoal.

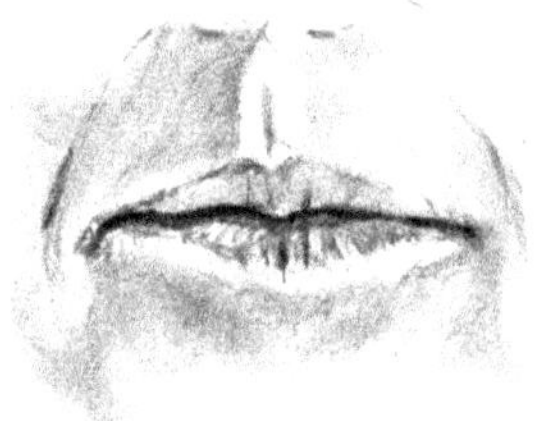

Shade in the general areas of shadow. Notice how the upper lip is slightly darker than the bottom lip.

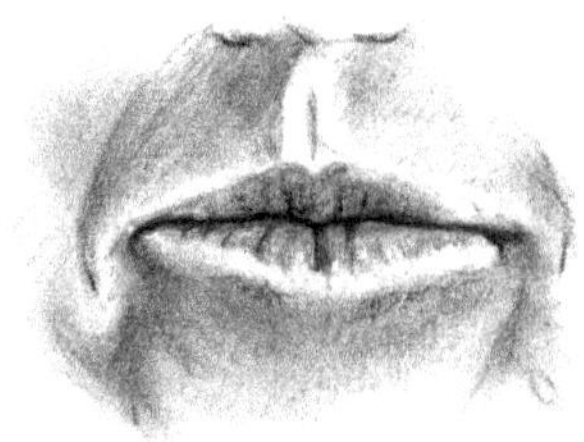

Begin to define the wrinkles and areas of shadow. Try to add more volume to the entire area.

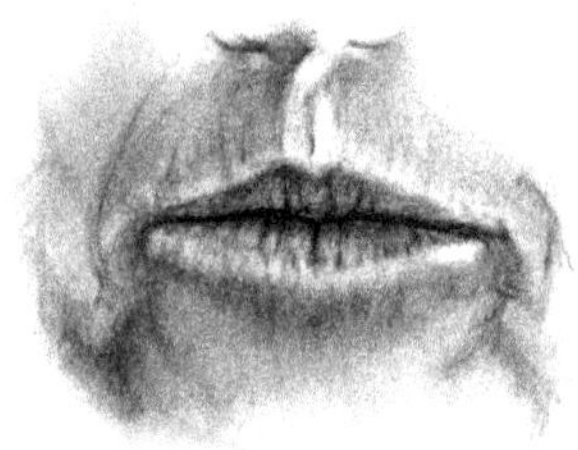

Continue to render skin tones, details, and wrinkles as well as textures of the lip using a little bit of compressed charcoal and mostly vine charcoal.

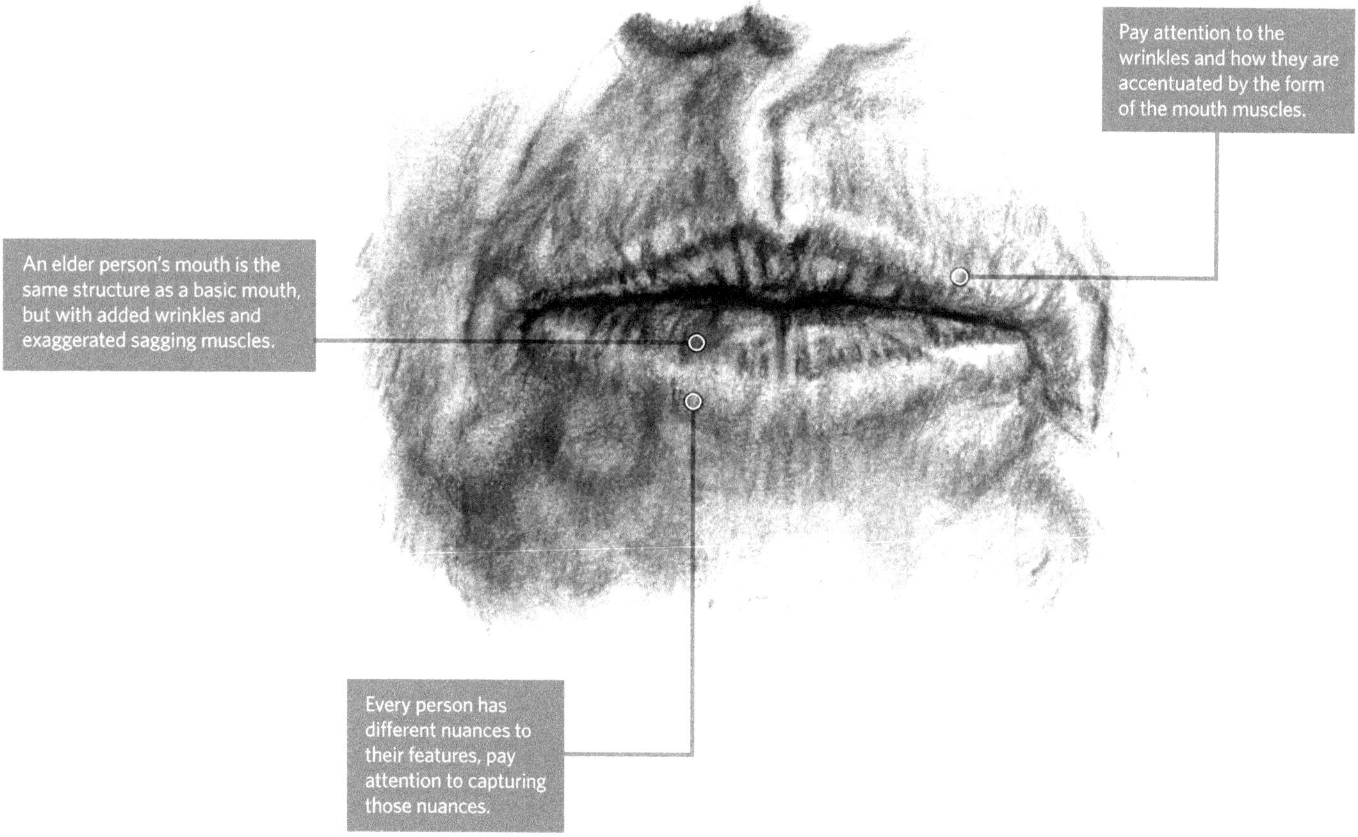

Pay attention to the wrinkles and how they are accentuated by the form of the mouth muscles.

An elder person's mouth is the same structure as a basic mouth, but with added wrinkles and exaggerated sagging muscles.

Every person has different nuances to their features, pay attention to capturing those nuances.

Now try drawing the elderly mouth yourself.

Now that you have practiced how to draw an old lady's mouth in charcoal following a step-by-step tutorial, use the page on the right to try and draw from life. You can draw from the picture below, use a mirror, or ask a friend to sit for you and try different variations of compositions.

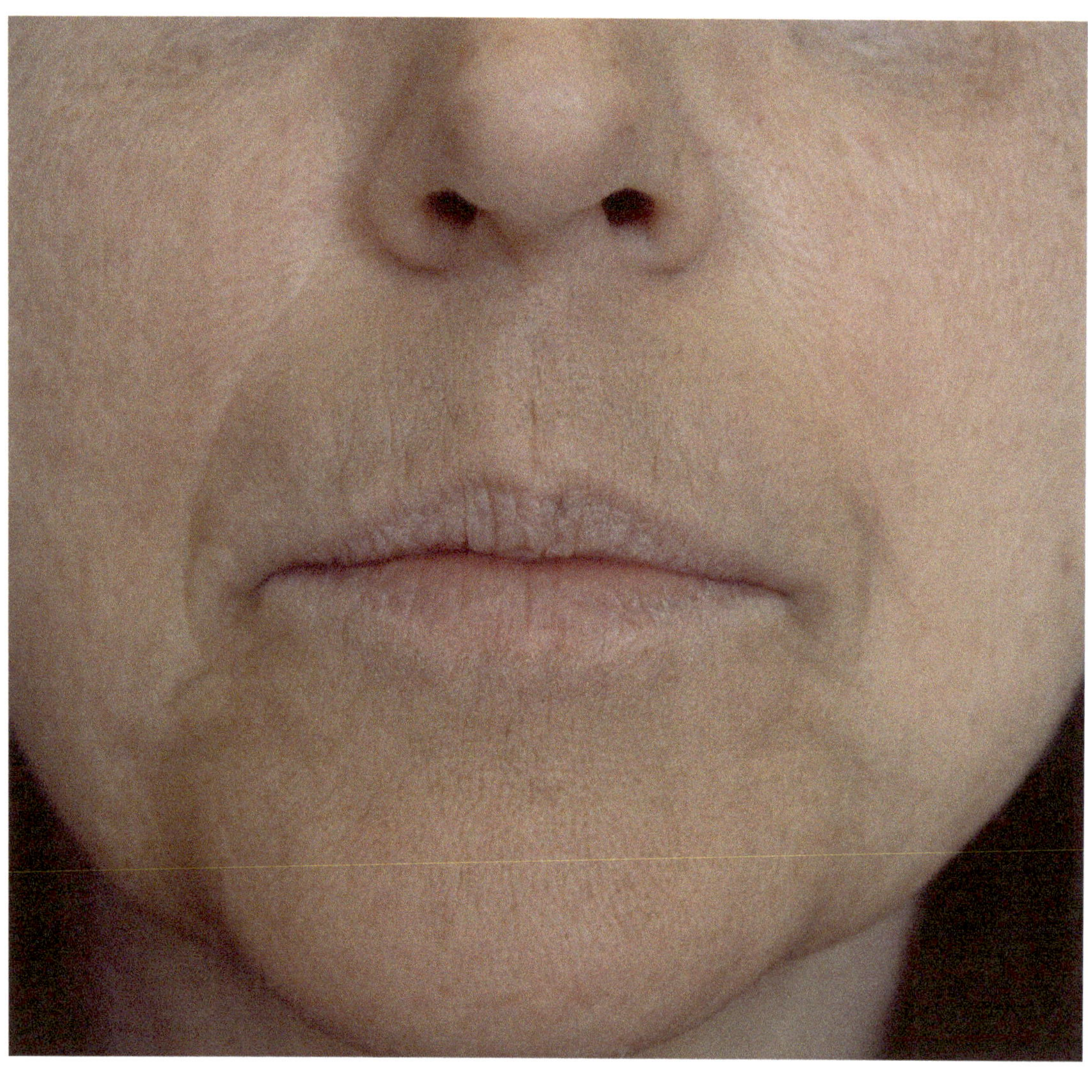

Now try drawing the elderly mouth yourself without the grid.

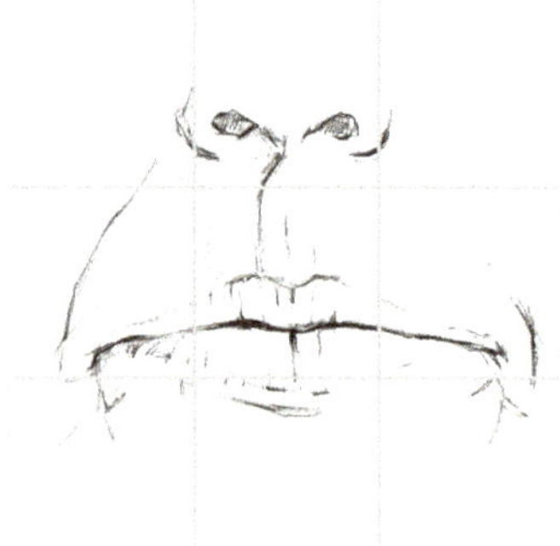

Draw the general lines to describe the shape of the lips and mouth area, as well as the frown line with vine charcoal.

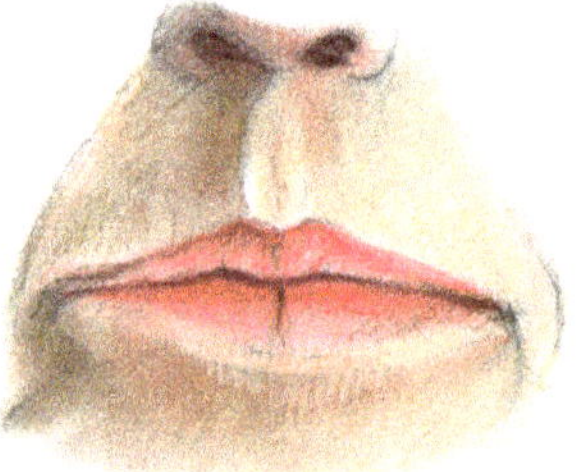

Shade in the general areas of shadow using warm skin tones and reds for the lips.. Notice how the upper lip is slightly darker than the bottom lip.

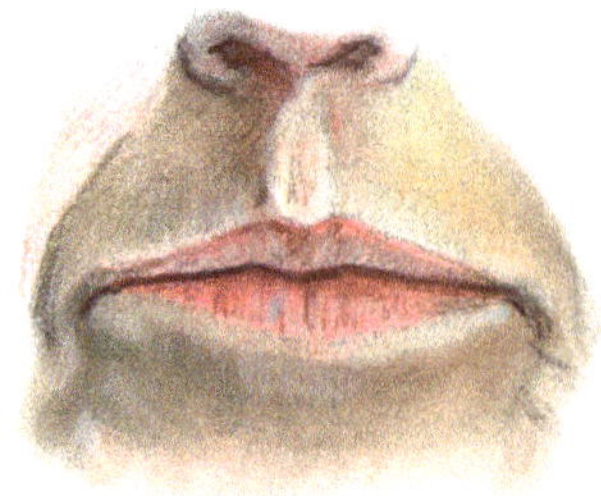

Using greens, blues and browns, render shadows. Use warm tones for highlights.

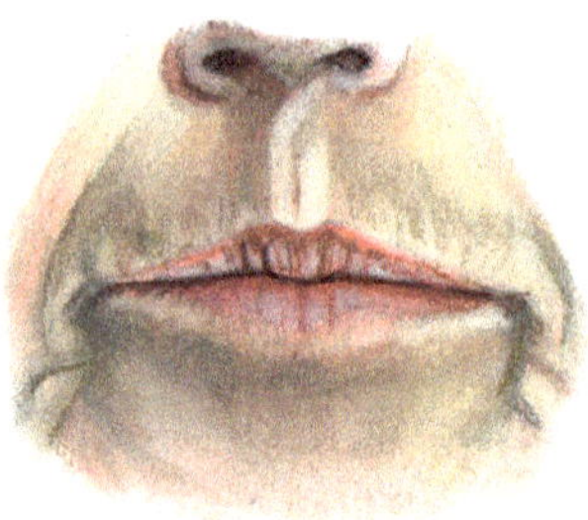

Continue to render skin tones as well as textures of the lip using more middle tones and greens, blues and browns. Smudge areas for a smoother texture.

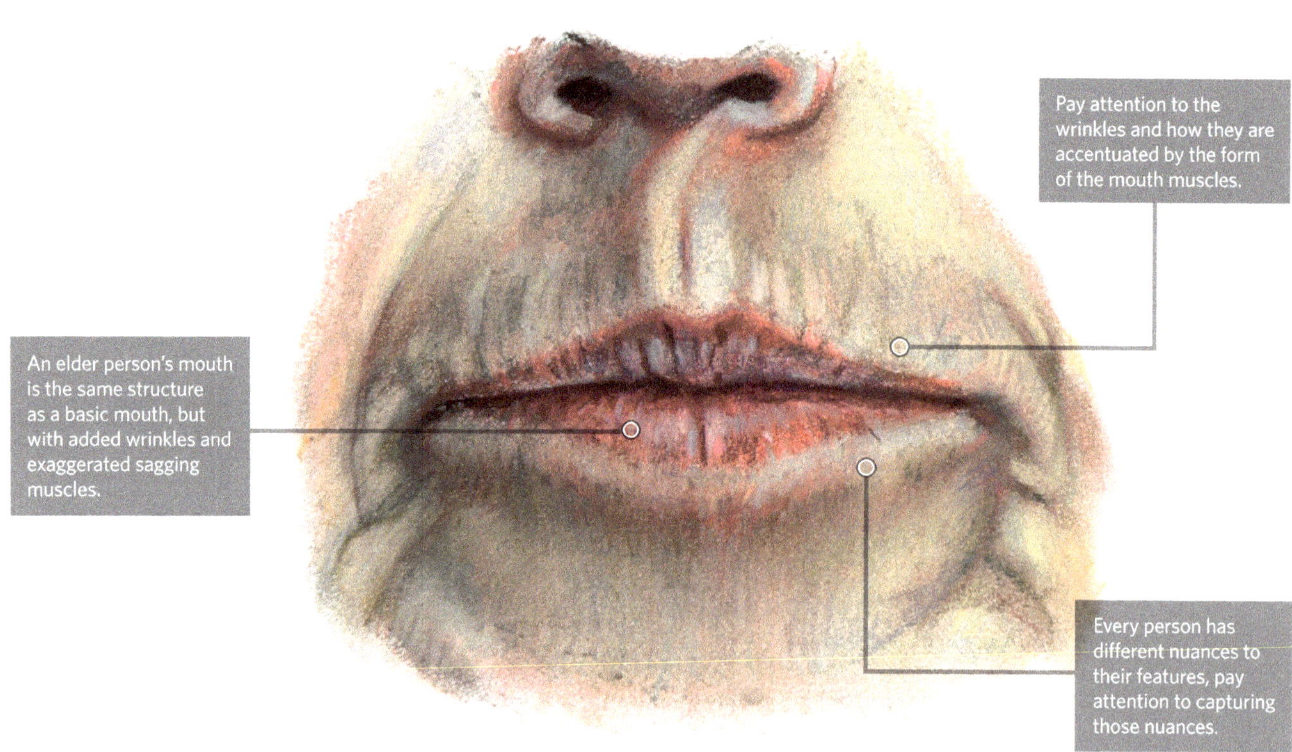

permanent red deep

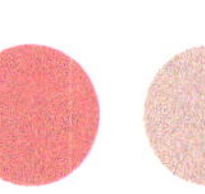
carmine

permanent red

light red oxide

permanent red light

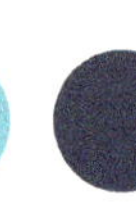
bluish green

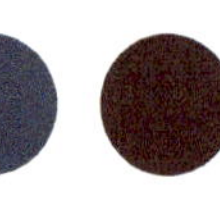
prussian blue

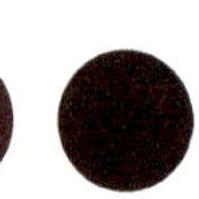
burnt umber

charcoal

white

Now try drawing the elderly mouth yourself.

Now that you have practiced how to draw an old lady's mouth in pastel following a step-by-step tutorial, use the page on the right to try and draw from life. You can draw from the picture below, use a mirror, or ask a friend to sit for you and try different variations of compositions.

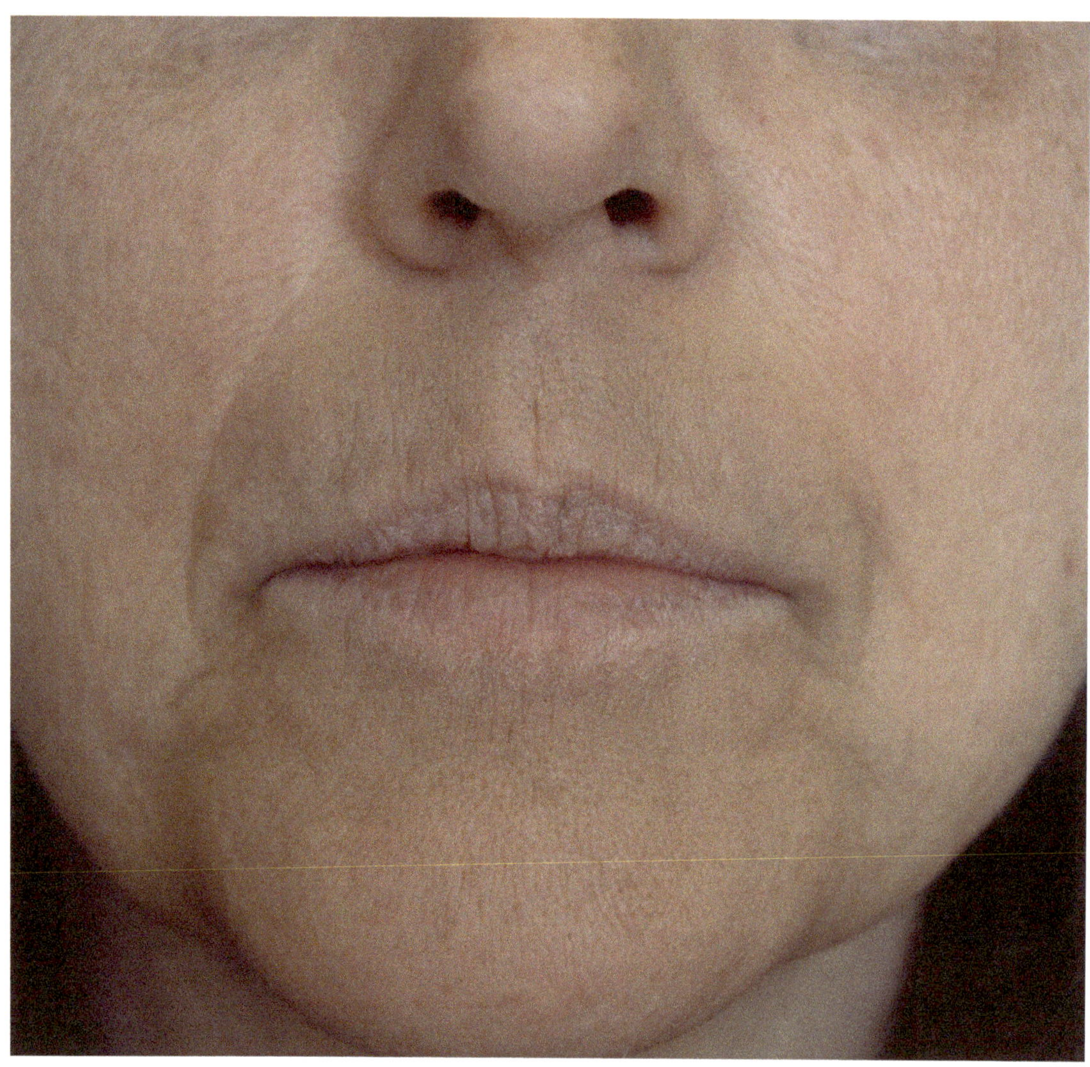

Now try drawing the elderly mouth yourself without the grid.

Now that you have practiced different ways the mouth can be drawn to express emotion and how light and shadow affect the mouth, try a couple of other perspectives. Pay attention to the shape of the lips in different perspectives, as well as the amount of flesh visible, the lips aren't always entirely visible depending on the angle.

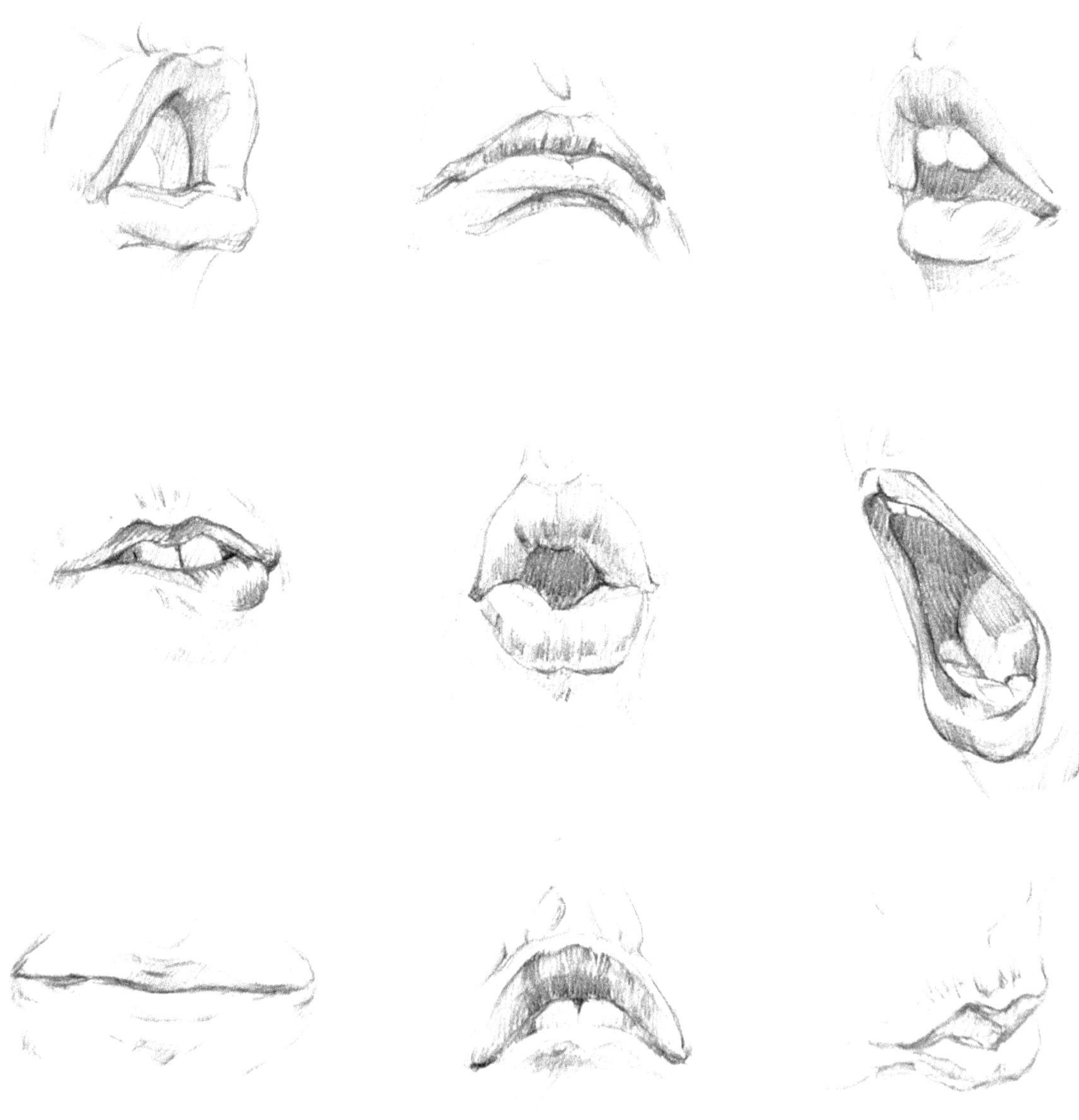

Now try drawing these basic mouth perspectives yourself.

ABOUT OOGIE HAUS

Oogie Haus is an art foundation unique for its diverse artistic endeavors, including an emphasis in art education, art & design internship opportunities, and volunteer outreach programs. There have been several book publications as well, such as "Art College Admissions," an insightful guideline for students applying to art schools.

Besides being an educational resource, Oogie Haus functions dually as an art gallery and art dealership. Through its research, it seeks to contribute a bigger network for local and international artists simultaneously curating its unique voice in todays art world. For more information please visit www.oogiehaus.com

ABOUT THE AUTHOR

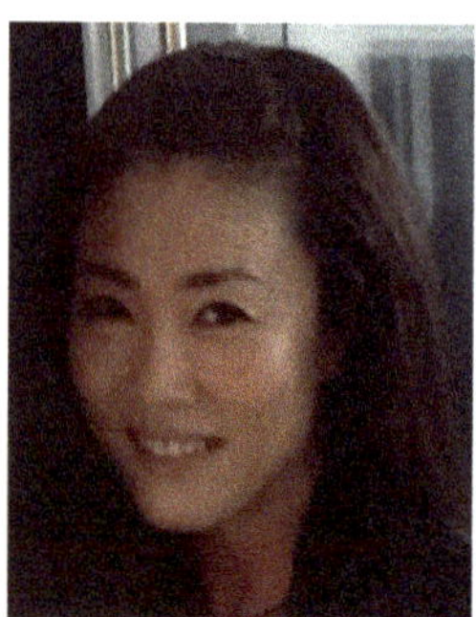

WOOK CHOI is an accomplished art dealer, education columnist, author, art educator, art gallerist, and art portfolio consultant who has guided over a thousand students to college admissions and scholarship success during the course of her 31-year teaching career.
She has received widespread recognition for her teaching methods from Mayor Michael Bloomberg; former First Lady Laura Bush; the New York Commissioner of Education, Richard P. Mills; US Congress member, Jerrold Nadler; the Alliance for Young Artists; YoungArts; and the Marie Walsh Sharpe Foundation. For more information, please visit www.wookchoi.com.

CHECK OUT SOME OF OUR OTHER BOOKS

ART COLLEGE ADMISSIONS

AN INSIDER'S GUIDE TO ART PORTFOLIO PREPARATION, SELECTING THE RIGHT COLLEGE AND GAINING ADMISSION WITH SCHOLARSHIPS

WOOK CHOI

ART COLLEGE ADMISSIONS

An insider's guide to portfolio preparation, selecting the right college and gaining admission with scholarships.
In the first half of this book, you'll learn how vital a role art plays in the success of businesses today, what admissions committees at top art colleges really look for when deciding who to admit, and essential tips for developing award-winning art portfolio pieces. In the second half, you'll learn about the distinct advantages and histories of the most highly-ranked and popular art colleges in the Northeast, specific and actionable tips for getting into each school, and any changes these schools have made to their admissions criteria in recent years.

YOU CAN CONTINUE TO DEVELOP YOUR ARTISTIC SKILLS IN DIFFERENT MEDIA!

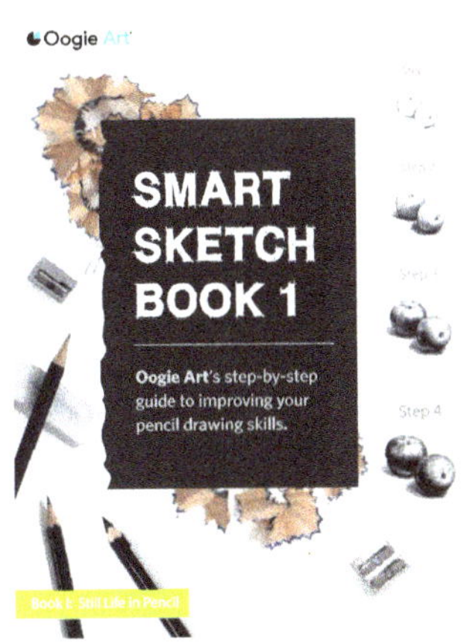

SMART SKETCHBOOK 1:
Still Life in Pencil

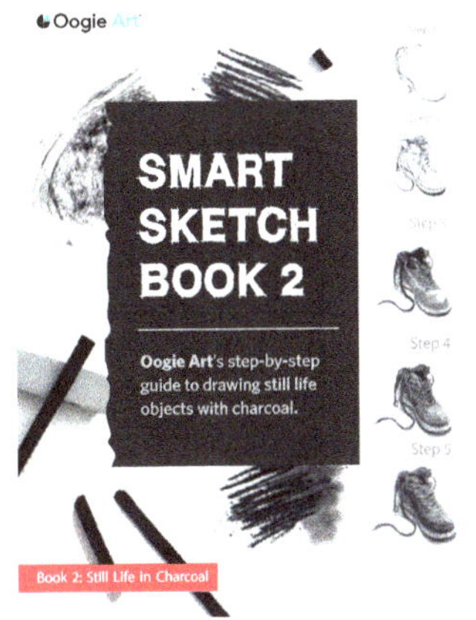

SMART SKETCHBOOK 2:
Still Life in Charcoal

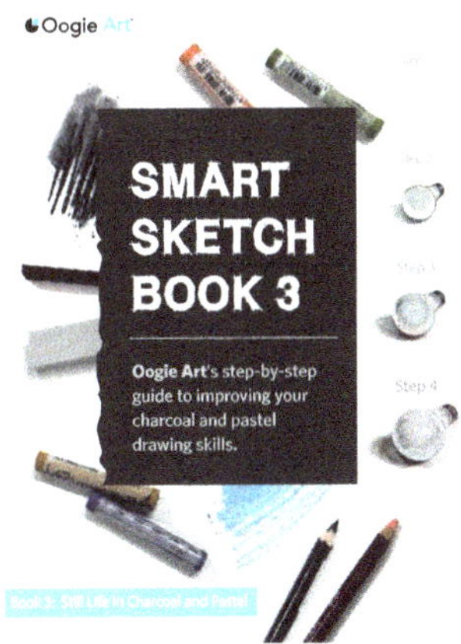

SMART SKETCHBOOK 3:
Still Life in Charcoal and Pastel

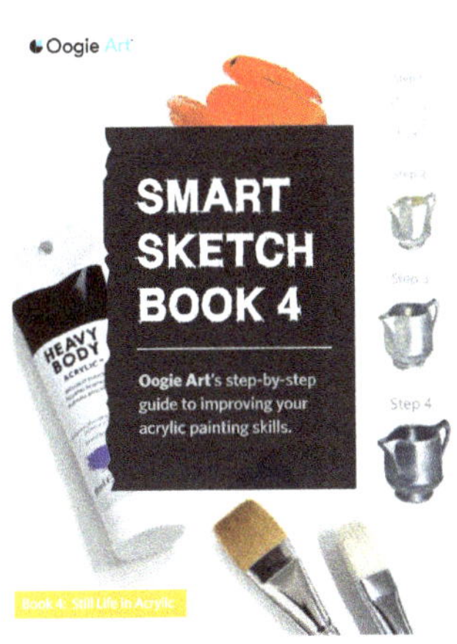

SMART SKETCHBOOK 4:
Still Life in Acrylic

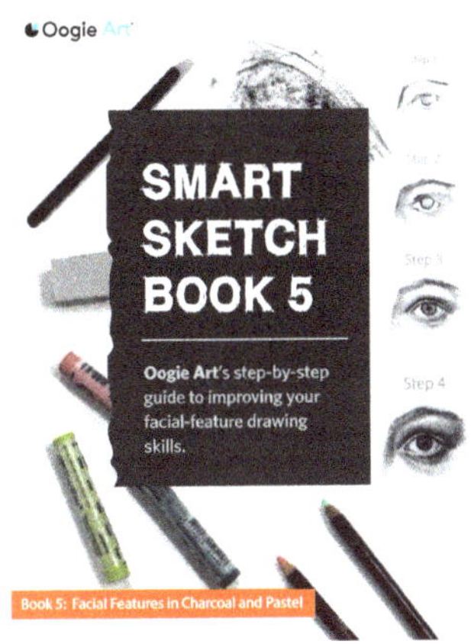

SMART SKETCHBOOK 5:
Facial Features in Charcoal and Pastel

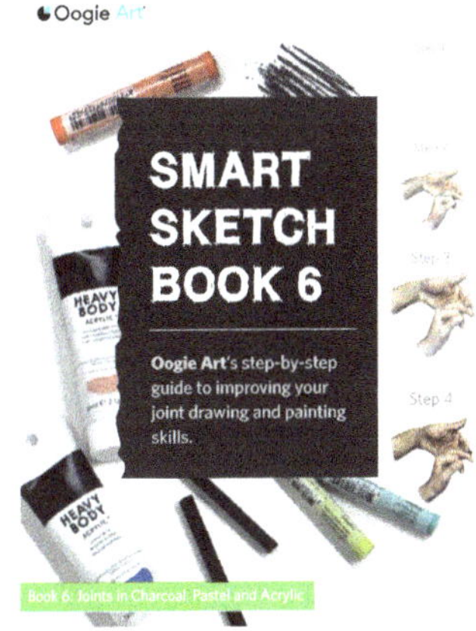

SMART SKETCHBOOK 6:
Joints in Charcoal, Pastel and Acrylic

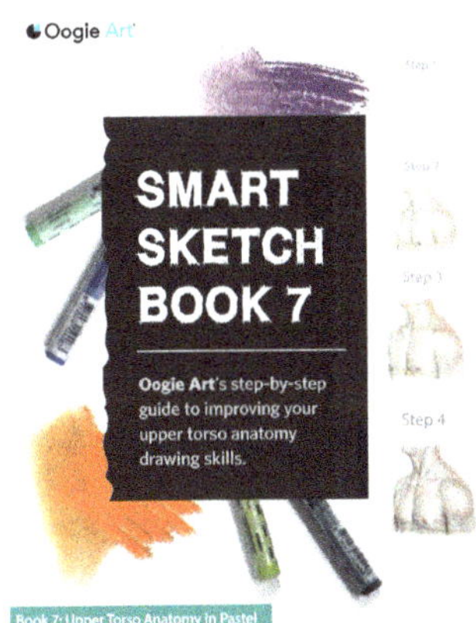

SMART SKETCHBOOK 7:
Upper Torso Anatomy in Pastel

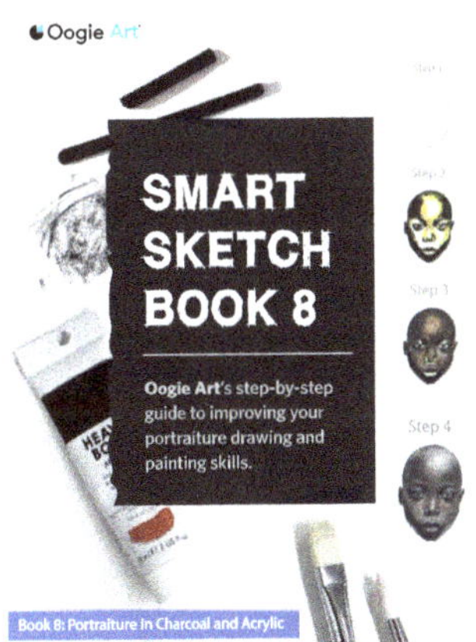

SMART SKETCHBOOK 8:
Portraiture in Charcoal and Acrylic

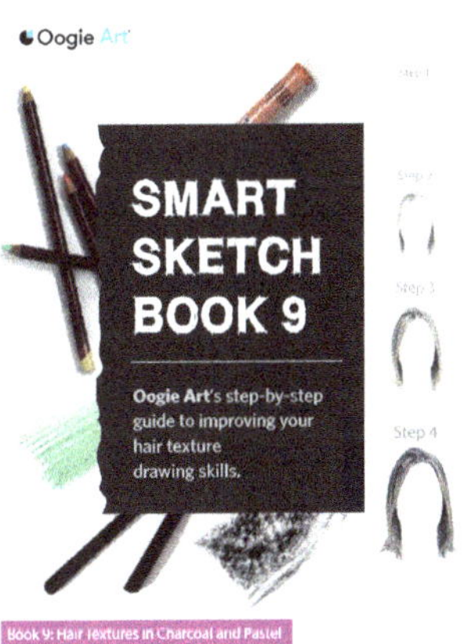

SMART SKETCHBOOK 9:
Hair Textures in Charcoal and Pastel

www.ingramcontent.com/pod-product-compliance
Ingram Content Group UK Ltd.
Pitfield, Milton Keynes, MK11 3LW, UK
UKHW062009290726
14090UKWH00022B/1471